Praise for *Simmering*

Orchant's book has a scattered structure and often a light tone. However, an engaging seriousness underlies it all. Some moments are disturbing, such as an account of a sexual assault she experienced at a party. There are also many moving meditations about life in these pages throughout ... Orchant will make readers appreciate food, family, and friends a bit more, and portrays life in general as a messy, sad, joyous, funny, and annoying mixture. A nourishing and easily digestible chronicle.

Kirkus Reviews

In *Simmering,* Rebecca Orchant is your bestie at a queer dinner party – an irreverent, bisexual, snickering pal who talks about ass while pouring the wine. Every chapter feels like an anecdote shared over a drink (maybe her "Aviation Cocktail," described as a "mouthful of flowers"). These vignettes about her life, food, sex, and pain are punctuated with truly tempting recipes, but the stories themselves are the real gems of this book, reminding readers of the strange alchemy between eating and remembering. A haunting prose poem about sexual assault and a devastating essay on death are tucked in with a recipe for preparing Cornish hens. The result is not a cookbook but an ode to cooking, a joyful and carnal ritual that bookends our best and worst days. Orchant zooms in on this ritual and gives it the personal examination it deserves.

Alexander Cheves

Simmering
A Kitchen Memoir

Simmering Rebecca Orchant

UNBOUND EDITION PRESS

Atlanta

FIRST EDITION

Printed in the United States of America

LIBRARY OF CONGRESS RECORD

Name: Orchant, Rebecca, 1984 — author.
Title: Simmering / Rebecca Orchant.
Edition: First edition.
Published: Atlanta : Unbound Edition Press, 2024.

LCCN: 2023947808
LCCN Permalink: https://lccn.loc.gov/2023947808
ISBN: 979-8-9892333-2-8 (fine softcover)

Designed by Eleanor Safe and Joseph Floresca
Printed by Bookmobile, Minneapolis, MN
Distributed by Itasca Books

123456789

Unbound Edition Press
1270 Caroline Street, Suite D120
Box 448
Atlanta, GA 30307

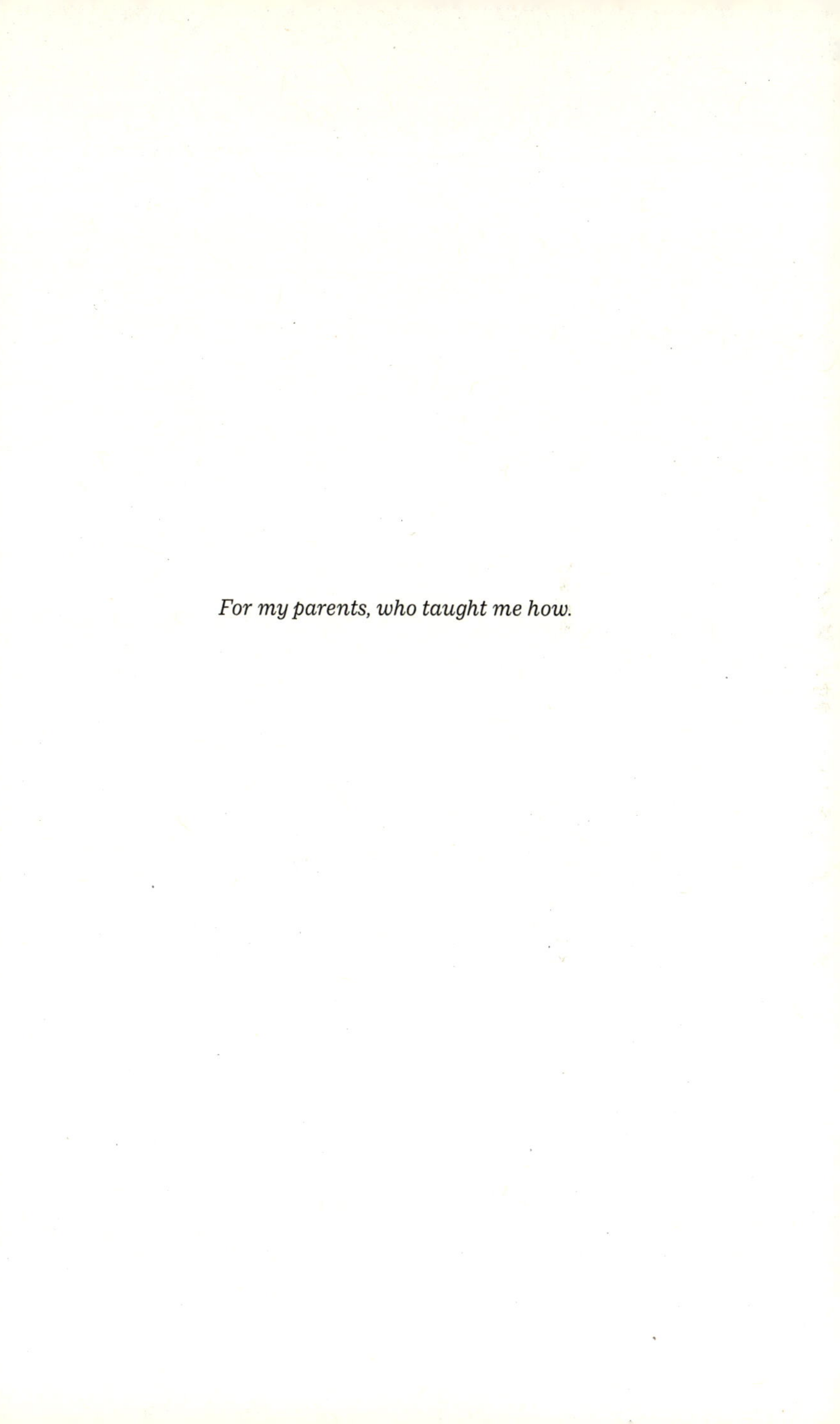

For my parents, who taught me how.

Contents

II.

III.

Simmering

Keepers of private notebooks are a different breed altogether, lonely and resistant rearrangers of things, anxious malcontents, children afflicted apparently at birth with some presentiment of loss.

JOAN DIDION

"Would you rather have sex or a radish?"
"If it were good sex I would rather have sex, but if it were bad sex I would rather have a radish."

MIRIAM MARGOLYES

To bake a cake in the eye of a storm; to feed yourself sugar on the cusp of danger.

OCEAN VUONG

Welcome to the Party

There's something to it: the way we flock to the kitchen at a party. What brings us there? Sometimes it's anxiety — when I can't handle small talk, I like to have a job making drinks, or assembling a cheese plate, or getting the table set. Sometimes it's an escape — my uncle is talking about the stock market again, so I need to go wash some dishes. Sometimes it's voyeurism — I want to see how the sausage gets made, literally and figuratively. Sometimes it's clarifying — does your brain work better when your hands are busy too?

In my little house in Provincetown, my kitchen is just another quadrant of the broader living space — downstairs is all one big room. You enter the house through the tiniest front door you've ever seen, just next to an inadequately slender fridge. The couch and the shelves of books and records flank the far end, across from the fireplace and TV. The sink and kitchen island lead you to the dining table dead in the middle of the room. Even still, while I'm standing on the hideous hunter green tile I would change in a heartbeat if I owned the place, I can trick my brain into thinking I'm in a different room — "in the kitchen." When people come over for dinner, while I finish the sauce, or rotate the Thanksgiving sides through the miniature oven, or stir the cocktail, I'm in my workspace until I want to drop into the conversation at the table.

"Rebecca, is there anything I can do to help?" People (including my husband Sean) often ask. The answer is usually "No" — not because I don't trust them, not because I don't want them in the kitchen with me, but because I do everything I can before they get there to make their time in my house labor-free.

When people come to our house, I want them to luxuriate. I want them to drink (if that's an option for them), I want them to snack, I want them to recline in their seats like someone is about to feed them a cluster of grapes by hand. And for some reason, while they're doing that, I want to work. I want to open the next bottle of wine just before the last glass has been poured out of the first one. I want to warm the bowls up with a ladleful of cooking water before I serve the pasta. I want to remember who wants cheese on top and who doesn't. I want to carve the turkey because everyone's afraid of it, to cut the first slice of pie. I want to know what you want before you want it.

When you come to our house, there's always something on the table to snack on, even if it's just a dish of olives and a piece of cheese. To call this a compulsion would indicate that it requires work or thought — the snack on the table before dinner is an extension of my consciousness. Sometimes it feels like it just appears. The snack on the table before dinner is a reflexive alchemy of the kitchens and the people who have shaped me and taught me how to love.

I guess what I'm trying to say is: This is the story of where the olives come from.

I.

Brooklyn: Shrimp and Grits

Sean and I have had a lot of kitchens together. I don't have a favorite; I think that would be impossible to decide. We've had kitchens that have cost us too much money, kitchens that have made us some, kitchens where we've sniped at each other, kitchens where we've tended to each other, kitchens where we've made love, kitchens where we've fucked each other nearly to death, kitchens where we've learned something new about the other person, and always where we've learned something about ourselves.

When we started dating, I had my first apartment kitchen, in an awful Albuquerque complex with identical stucco buildings, and a balcony that overlooked the dismal strip-mall wasteland of San Mateo Boulevard. I always thought I'd sit out there and drink tea, or some bullshit, but mostly it was used as a place for drunk people to vomit with a view of the rollercoaster at Cliff's Amusement Park. It was my last year of college, and although I could feel adult responsibility gunning for me, I was still just beyond its reach.

The first time I invited Sean over for dinner, I wanted to make it clear that I loved him, which I knew from the second I met him, although it would take us a few years to get from me knowing that to us really doing it. We spent those years sitting next to each other in classes — he'd bring me a grilled cheese or a carne adovada burrito from the diner across the street, and I'd save him a chair. He was funnier and smarter than anyone in the class, but only our teachers and I seemed to realize it. We were both in serious relationships when we met, which we watched end of their own accord from our separate, platonic bleachers, until finally it seemed like it was our time to give it a try.

Before he arrived, I cut radishes in half and smeared them with sweet butter and fat, flaky salt ("It was lavender salt," he reminds me). I cooked grits gently over a makeshift double-boiler for hours, and poached shrimp in tomato sauce, rich with ribbons of prosciutto and white wine. We sat at the breakfast nook, because my dining room only had a beer pong table in it, and talked about how nice it was to already know how much we liked each other. I remember thinking that my parents were going to be really excited about him. I don't remember if I made dessert, because we were officially in love after the first bite. I do remember going out to the balcony where he was sitting after dinner, putting his head in my hands and asking if he wanted to go to bed, like we'd already done it a thousand times before. After shrimp and grits, we never stopped.

We burned mix tapes full of pirated MP3s onto CDs, labeled with clever references to inside jokes about the curious, tender, gratifying love we were finally making. We shopped for records and second-hand books, and I introduced him to every friend I'd ever had. Once he got his own apartment in Albuquerque, I stayed there so much my roommate got startled anytime I came home.

Our first kitchen together was the one in the old Albuquerque High School. We lived in a loft apartment, the kind that absorbed old paper mills and other huge, abandoned buildings like a virus in the mid-2000s. We had 15-foot-high windows, 20-foot ceilings, a chalkboard leftover from our apartment's former life as the principal's office, and more kitchen space than I've ever had, before or since. Most of our furniture was his, since he'd recently gotten divorced, and I'd just barely moved out of my parents' house. We slept in his queen-size bed, which felt extremely luxurious. There was a silly little loft, that you could only get up to by ladder and definitely couldn't stand up in, which we used for storage, and as a writing and editing nook. Once, when I was struggling to finish the last play I ever wrote, he dragged a bunch of blankets up there and made me a little nest that he continually delivered cups of tea and tiny cheese plates up to while I worked. I'd never dated another writer before, and I decided then that this was the only way to live.

That apartment is the only place I ever lived in Albuquerque that had anything resembling a walking neighborhood, and we used to walk home with all of our friends from drinks at The Anodyne, grabbing a whole pizza along the way, hosting the afterparty like freshly graduated morons without a care in the world. We were both working jobs that felt very grown up, but definitely weren't, making an adorable little income but living like kings, and I think that if my dad hadn't died, we would have had a very hard time leaving.

But he did, and so we left. In part, to get our heads straight after what we'd just experienced, but also because I was afraid that if we didn't do it then, we never would.

We crash-landed through a few more kitchens — his dad and stepmom, Jack and Beth's, in Santa Fe, where we tried to distract ourselves by making homemade mayonnaise with a whisk and ended up with something closer to polymer. Then Jack and Beth's again on Cape Cod, where I baked my first all-by-myself challah because I couldn't find any at the Chatham Village Market for Rosh Hashanah. While we were there, we worked at a sandwich shop called the Chatham Cookware, run by a buxom, brash bisexual named Rebecca.

She let us work the sandwich line and make deli salads in gigantic proportions in the kitchen, and she barely yelled at me when I burned the barley for the beet salad for the eighth time that summer because my brain was so frazzled. She'd also lost her dad recently, and I think we recognized each other as kindred spirits right away. Had we not spent that summer memorizing sandwich ingredients and hosing down anti-slip mats out back, our own Provincetown shop, Pop+Dutch, might never have existed.

After that, we went on to Brooklyn — our first kitchen on Baltic Street was so infested with cockroaches from the laundromat below us, that I will never use a drip coffee maker ever again. We were unemployed and terrified, because it was November 2008, and no one was sure if there would ever be another job to get. But we found plentiful bowls of hand-pulled noodles in Chinatown within our budget, and finally got to experience the joys of a serious farmer's market. That disgusting apartment was also a place of great friendship, where we co-hosted our first Passover Seder with a brilliant glutton we called Dr. Booze (who would go on to officiate our wedding), and where I first slid the cocktail and dish of warm, roasted olives in front of my dear friend Flynn that she has referenced so many times since. Flynn would go on to become my writing partner, my forever editor, and one of the best friends I've ever had. She works harder than anyone I know and uses the spoils to disperse treats far and wide. "There is," she says often, "no point in me doing all this capitalism if we can't all enjoy it."

I wish I hadn't had to find a cockroach leg in my coffee to get to this point, but we don't get to choose our journey.

We fled Baltic Street for Atlantic Avenue, where we rented an L-shaped studio apartment above a Middle Eastern restaurant that baked fresh pita. The oven was so hot that the hallway on the other side of it was always warm. Our sleep in that apartment was regulated by the B63 bus, which stopped directly outside our window every 20 minutes, and by the hissing radiators on either end of the room. We had a bathroom with a big window and a bathtub, and in the long kitchen between the bathroom and the living area, there was the only functioning garbage disposal I've ever had.

Once a year there is an enormous block party — The Atlantic Antic — where restaurants and businesses up and down the block set up outside tents, tables, dance floors, and other parties. There was a Spanish restaurant down the street that brought out a 20-foot-long iron grill, lined from end to end with fresh sardines and chorizo on skewers. There were aguas frescas, and zeppole, and you were allowed to drink beers in the street. The French restaurant on the other side of our apartment had Kronenbourg on tap, and would always roast a whole pig, the head of which I somehow managed to charm them into giving to us free of charge. We sat with our legs dangling out the windows, drinking beers with our friends, picking at the roasted pig's head and whatever other treats we'd amassed, playing music loudly enough that revelers in the street would dance their way past. This one day a year in south Brooklyn is the closest I've ever gotten to living in New Orleans.

The Atlantic kitchen was where I fermented pickles for the first time, where I decided to start a project of cooking through an entire book of canapes and hors d'oeuvres from the 1920s and writing about them. It is where Sean and I had our first absolute kitchen disaster — trying to make pasta from scratch for the first time with under-hydrated, under-rested pasta dough. That ended in tears on the floor and Chinese take-out. It was also where, one day in March of 2010, Sean announced that he was planning to make us dinner. He seared steaks and made braised leeks and white beans with crème fraîche and white wine, and as he sat down to eat, he slipped his kitchen shoes — then, bright purple Crocs — off under the table.

"Why did you just take your shoes off?" I asked, bemused.

"Because I didn't want to propose to you wearing Crocs," he said, just before he pulled a delicate diamond solitaire engagement ring out of his pocket and bent down on one knee.

I shut up for as long as I possibly could before the "yes, yes, yes, of course!" jumped out of my mouth. We finished the meal laughing, crying, drinking cocktails and calling everyone we loved to tell them the news.

We planned our wedding in less than five months, eager to get past planning the pomp and circumstance (that's a hilarious thing to say about an event of 80 people at a house in Truro, where we ate pickles during the ceremony and drank 40 ounce beers on the dance floor) and into the rest of our lives together. We made sure there were radishes with butter and salt at the reception.

We had a conversation the other day about whether or not, if we had to decide now, we'd choose to get married — or, as we've most recently been referring to it, "getting the government involved." We've learned so much in the years following about our love for each other, and which commitments are really important, that we both agreed we wouldn't think it was necessary. But I'm glad we jumped into that decision those years ago — it was a great fucking party. It's funny to think that a wedding is usually the "happy ending" of a romantic story. For us, the most challenging, most rewarding, and most amazing times were absolutely still to come.

Grits for Wooing a Great Love

5 cups water
1 cup stone-ground grits (or polenta will work too)
3 tsp. kosher salt, or to taste
2 Tbsp. butter, or to taste

In a bowl, cover the grits with an inch or two of cold water and stir them vigorously. Let them settle for a minute or two and skim off any chaff floating at the top. Strain the water off through a fine, mesh sieve. (You can skip this step if you're using regular grits or polenta.)

Bring the water to a simmer in a large saucepan. Whisk in the grits, then stir constantly until the water returns to a simmer. Reduce the heat until the grits only sputter occasionally like a cartoon tar pit, and cook, uncovered, for about 1 hour, stirring every time you think of them, until thick but still fluid. If they get too stiff, add a dash of water. Add salt and a generous dose of butter. Taste, and add more if you like.

Transfer the pan to a double boiler set over simmering water and cover tightly (you can set a circle of parchment paper directly onto the top of the grits if your lid doesn't fit the saucepan perfectly). Allow the grits to rest that way for *at least* 30 minutes — or up to a few hours, depending on your timing. If you don't have a double boiler (I don't), you can rig a makeshift version by setting the saucepan containing the grits on a small, ovenproof ramekin centered inside a wider, deeper pot, and surrounding it with barely simmering water. Keep a kettle of warm water on hand to top the water level off as needed.

Serve hot, on their own, or topped with tomato poached shrimp, your favorite ragu, pulled pork — go nuts, fall in love.

Serves 4 — 6

Braised Leeks and White Beans

2 leeks, sliced and rinsed twice
A few sprigs of fresh thyme, leaves stripped
2 cloves garlic, peeled and minced
2 Tbsp. olive oil
2 Tbsp. butter
A glass of white wine (about 1 ½ cups)
1 15.5oz can cannellini or butter beans, drained and rinsed
A small handful of flat-leaf parsley, finely chopped
1 Tbsp. crème fraîche (or sour cream)
Kosher salt and black pepper

In a heavy-bottomed saucepan, melt the butter with the olive oil over low heat. Add the leeks and thyme with a pinch of salt, and sweat for 20 minutes, until the leeks are soft. Add the garlic and cook for a few minutes until it smells good. Turn the heat up to medium and add the wine. Let it come to a boil, then add the beans and a splash of water, so that the beans are almost covered with liquid. Simmer for 10 minutes, until the beans start to get creamy (I like to mash a few up with the wooden spoon I'm using to stir). Add the parsley, crème fraîche (or sour cream), another glug of olive oil, and a few grinds of black pepper.

Serve hot, with sliced, medium-rare ribeyes over the top — if you're trying to get engaged or something.

Serves 2

Provincetown: Toasty

When I announced my departure from *The Huffington Post* for Provincetown, a colleague chimed in on the long, tender, "we'll miss you" email thread: "I don't know whether you already have a drinking problem or not, but Provincetown in the winter is a great place to get one."

This far-flung land of salt spray and queerdom is well-known for debauchery, one of the things that drew us here in the first place. I knew there would be alcohol, I knew there would be parties, I knew there would be indulgence, but I didn't realize I was going to fucking fall in love with a fisherman.

Where to begin here? This is a story I've begun to tell many times before — because it's easy to meet Daniil and see how you could become sexually obsessed with him. He is lithe, nimble, strong, full of energy, with the face of a cherub and the forearms of Poseidon. Once you talk with him, it's easy to see how you could become emotionally obsessed with him, too. He is funny, fiercely interested, smarter than he protests, and has a Belarusian accent that makes everything sound like it's been filtered through dark wildflower honey. But once all that flows, ebbs, falls away, changes, evolves into another feeling altogether, you fall in love, date, break up, wash, rinse, repeat. There is one thing that always remains — he is really fucking great at feeding us.

We have the kind of meals at his house that you look back on afterward, magic hanging in the air like smoke from the woodstove and think — *those were the days* — even if it was just yesterday.

Let's start with the crabs. It was summer, which meant I was exhausted from work and probably feeling a little anti-social. He invited Sean and me to his house for the first time, to have dinner and watch a movie projected onto a sheet outside. It was one of those days, over Labor Day weekend if I remember correctly, when all I wanted to do was sleep, lick my wounds, and get ready for the next round of summertime sandwich shop battle. But the siren song of food that someone else makes for you proved to overtake all those feelings, and we found ourselves standing in his beautiful house.

Daniil lives in a magical place — a family-owned, charmingly ramshackle hill in the woods that time, care, and town government somehow forgot. The hill is peppered with shacks, in addition to a few larger, main structures. His house — Toasty, as we've now come to refer to it, since his woodstove operates somewhere near the temperature of the sun all winter — is a free-standing cottage on the side of the hill furthest from town. He has a talent for woodwork, which becomes immediately apparent the moment you step on the property. Everywhere you turn, wood of all types and textures and colors has been measured, sanded, and fit into place along the walls, inlaid in closet doors, on the floor. Despite his rustic themes, he has a modern aesthetic, the furniture is clean, comfortable, and spare. You are never inside for more than five minutes before being offered a drink, a snack. It is, I think, how people must feel when they come to my house for dinner, which makes me feel really proud.

On this particular night, all those years ago, he'd prepared a gigantic, steaming pot of blue crabs, pulled up from the water hours before, in a spicy, pungent broth. The crabs are always bruisers, with claws uncrackable by human hands, for which Daniil handily wields a literal hatchet. There were bottles and bottles of rosé, a casual cheese board, friends, twinkle lights, and Margot and Richie Tenenbaum holding each other in a tent on screen. It was the second moment I realized my crush on him was not going away.

I've lost count of how many of those times I've had at this point, but there are a few that stand out in particular.

There was the time Dori made us razor clam ceviche, with chiles and cilantro and citrus, all minced up and piled back into the clam shells. We all stood around the counter eating them the second they were ready. Daniil put the whole shell in his mouth and pulled it back out absolutely clean, his eyes glinting.

There was the time he, without warning, made us a shuba salad in the dead of winter. Shuba, also called "Herring Under a Fur Coat," which is about the most Russian thing I can think of, is a layered spectacle of preserved herring wrapped in grated potato, carrots and beets, with a robe of mayonnaise. I'd only ever seen one of these in my mind, until he made it for us. It was a perfect, beautiful, dome: the beets and mayo mixed together to make the loveliest shade of pink. We made him walk us through the construction, step by step.

"The herring," he explained, "should never touch the mayonnaise."

"It's the most beautiful salad I've ever seen," I said.

"Well," he replied, "traditionally it's not a salad, it's a chaser." And he refilled my wine glass.

There are always Syrniki — Russian farmer's cheese pancakes, laced with vanilla sugar and just enough egg and flour to hold them together. They're like if you patted the inside of a blintz into a little disc and pan-fried it in butter. They demand cherry preserves and sour cream. I have never cared much for sweets in the morning, but these blur the line by being another excellent excuse to eat cheese for breakfast. A plate of Syrniki will also keep you full and warm for an entire day's work in the garden, or a morning of sledding in the dunes.

Recently, at a chosen-family dinner, we were talking about how eating too many dried apricots can wreak havoc on your stomach. Someone mentioned that it's because of the fiber, or the sorbitol, or something.

"Also, I think it has something to do with the fact that you wouldn't eat, like, a dozen fresh apricots in one sitting like you do dried ones."

"Oh, Rebecca," he said wistfully with a smirk, "How can you know so little about me still?"

Daniil (or Squirrel, Daniila, Danik, DZ, Danny Scallops, Buddy, among a million other nicknames I've hoarded into my heart for this dear, dear creature) is my favorite kind of dining companion. He is always up for a stupid idea, like getting twice as many appetizers as there are people at the table. He will always drink a bottle of wine at lunch with me, and frequently suggests a little whiskey in our coffee at breakfast, just to get the day started with a treat.

He is usually trying to put on a show in his kitchen, because he really can't help himself but be entertaining. Sometimes I like it even better when he's too tired for that. Living and working in a summer-focused tourist town means that we've seen each other at our most exasperated, and one of my favorite ever memories of his kitchen comes from this point in time. This was toward the end of our romantic time together. We had both finished work and wanted to hang out but couldn't quite figure out what to do about it. I offered to get takeout.

"Do you have any mushrooms?" he asked.

"Yes, somehow," I said.

"What about an onion?"

"Always."

"Great, bring them. I have everything else."

I had no idea what I was in for, but I trusted him with my stomach way more than I did with my heart, so I did what he asked and drove the five minutes to his house, along with a raggedy bunch of dill from the crisper, and an overnight bag. It was fall, there was a chill in the air, but once I stepped inside Toasty, it didn't matter. The woodstove was crackling away, there was music in the air, and Daniil was shirtless in the kitchen — a deep breath of gratitude for getting to experience this moment more than once in my little life.

He poured me a glass of white wine, something I've never been interested in drinking in the cooler months until I dated this little weirdo, who danced his way around me into an embrace. Dinner, he confessed, was just what he wanted to eat when he was alone — which is to say, frozen pork pelmeni, with sauteed mushrooms, onions and sour cream on top. People of Earth: I say to you now, date a Belarusian if you love to eat. You will not be disappointed by the food.

"Oh, how perfect, I found some dill in my fridge," I said.

"Rivkah," he responded, truly the only person in the world to ever call me by my Hebrew name, "of course you did."

I took a picture of him that night, still shirtless, leaning over a steaming bowl of ground pork dumplings, with a pile of creamy vegetables on top. It might be one of my happiest memories of our romantic relationship. He was beaming, proud of himself, happy to be eating what he really wanted to anyway, happy to have someone who wanted to eat it with him, happy to be with me. It may be the most comfortable I've ever felt around him, and I'm sure we slept very well. I still have very romantic feelings about mushrooms and onions and sour cream.

Being in love with this person was like trying to grasp something underwater.

While I still love him very much and will probably never stop, we are no longer in love with each other — at least not all the time, and not in the impossibly messy way we were a few years ago. For a few years, he lived with a gorgeous woman who became one of my closest friends and kitchen bros, and is an unbelievable cook and weirdo in her own right.

Sofia cooks with a kind of fearlessness that always blows my mind. She doesn't shy away from technique or a challenge; the more steps the better. In the brief time I've known her, she's slid in front of me bowl after bowl of homemade wontons, Peking-style duck that she dried with a household fan for an entire day, homemade pelmeni, paella from a pan so big we had to cook it outside over a propane burner, so many galettes I've lost count, nearly perfect steamed pork buns on her first try, and a 12-layer Russian honey cake that seemed to defy gravity.

For a while, they made each other insanely happy, and also happily insane. In all honesty, I often missed getting to bury my face in his chest, but it never overshadowed my joy that they found each other. Their romantic relationship has since ended, but we all still occasionally feel like family. I'm proud every day of how we all co-exist, knowing what we know about how easily obsessed we can all be with one another.

Daniil's kitchen is one of the warmest places I've ever been, I mean that literally and figuratively. I've had some of the most vulnerable conversations of my adult life across that countertop, some of the horniest thoughts, some of the most tender glances. I've also laughed my ass off, drunk far too much wine, stared at the counter while I had nothing to say, and prepared some of the best food on Earth with some of the best people.

We often eat with our hands at the counter or on the deck out front, having cooked a two-inch thick steak and every vegetable we've pulled out of our respective gardens over a huge open fire. Oftentimes, there's a batched cocktail by Ben or Sean or me, occasionally one of us breaks a glass by accident. Always, always, there is the constant sound of laughter, the kind that makes your muscles ache and your eyes twinkle with tears. Under those lights, everyone looks even more beautiful than they are, and I always feel so lucky to be with them. Especially during the pandemic years, when so many folks were home alone, or cooped up in an apartment, scared and bored. We were often scared, but we were rarely bored, and I can't imagine my life without those people, that kitchen, and the things we've shared there.

Harwich: Honeynut

I am often misidentified as a straight person, because I happen to be married to a very tall, very handsome man. But I am, in fact, gay as hell, a proud and practicing polyamorous bisexual. This isn't something I've felt the need to clarify or promote for much of my life, especially after Sean and I got married and I felt like I'd made "my choice." That is, right up until I made Provincetown my home and began to realize that being married to a man didn't negate my queerness. Once he and I started experimenting with polyamory, I realized I could do a lot more than name my identity, I could very much continue to participate in shaping it. People often ask what I like the most about living in Provincetown, and my answer is always that it's a place where people come to be exactly themselves. This place has allowed me to find the fullest, lushest, most vibrant expression of who I am to date, and I'll be forever grateful to it for that.

Fumbling my way through a bisexual and polyamorous life experiment has taught me so much about myself, and other people. Through it, I've learned what kind of touch I like and how to articulate it with my whole throat, as often as I can (will be working on this one for as long as I'm alive, probably). I've learned *a lot* of vegetarian and vegan cooking techniques, and about the genius that is Bryant Terry. I've learned how to manage my own dizzying limerence with a partner's tender envy, and vice versa (will also be working on this one for the rest of my life). I've learned how to sleep with someone else's cat curled up on my hip. I've learned a lot about how much affection I have to give, how many people I can feed at once, and been humbled by pushing the boundaries of both.

I have also, importantly, learned that under the right circumstances, I really like to relinquish control to someone I trust, and to let them spank the ever-loving shit out of me.

I met a woman who loves apple sauce, *Dazed and Confused,* and kink — not definitely, but possibly, in that order. Alison and I have now been in each other's lives for many years, with varying levels of intensity and commitment, and I'm sure we'll be friends forever no matter what happens next. But I'm here to tell you about the kitchens of my life, and hers really can't go unremarked upon, because it is, gentle reader, where I was first tied to a ceiling beam and summarily slapped with a leather riding crop from neck to ankles.

I am an enthusiastic champion of the kink community, but have rarely had my own experiences within it, and came to this experience as a near-total newbie. When she invited me to her house for dinner that night, Alison mentioned that she'd like to experiment with some restraints and some impact play to see if I'd respond to it. I love when someone deftly devises a plan that involves both feeding me and fucking me, but I was also nervous about whether I'd like it or not.

I have long identified as a power bottom, and I can be a little indignant about relinquishing control. I needn't have worried, in this case.

We sat at the little two-person table in the kitchen of the house she was renting in Harwich and drank wine. She was simmering a stew of white beans, tomatoes, and vegetables on the stove, and her cat curled herself into my lap as we ate. She'd requested that I wear a dress, something "not too easy to take off, buttons, if possible," and I'd complied, wearing a red silk dress that's lined in pink satin, and pretty much never fails to get me railed. I was worried that I'd spill wine on it, or that her cat's claws would snag it, but it made it through dinner unscathed. We sat on her couch after dinner, legs tangled around each other, while she dragged her fingernails up and down my skin (a habit she indulges in any time my skin is within reach).

"Are you up for trying something new tonight?" she asked.

The few times we'd slept together had already improved my intimate vocabulary. She was the first person who ever asked what kind of touch I like, the first person who ever asked if I like penetration *before she did it,* the first person I ever fucked as an adult where it didn't feel like there was a default setting. If you're unacquainted with how hot enthusiastic consent can be, I hope that you find a queer person who wants to fuck you before the world ends.

Something new: a long, black nylon rope, slung over an exposed beam in the middle of the kitchen, then tied delicately but snugly around both my wrists.

"Does that feel too tight?" she asked.

"No."

"Does it feel tight enough?"

She turned the lights off and lit a few candles, which I was grateful for. Sometimes I'm bashful when the lights are too bright. She tied the rope off so that my arms were hoisted over my head and set to unbuttoning my dress.

"If anything starts to hurt or go numb, just tell me and we'll take a break."

I didn't know it before this experience, but I had always conflated impact play with degradation. The two are not inexorably linked and learning that they are separate enthusiasms that can be disentangled has been really good for me. I never want to be called a "good little girl," or a "dirty little slut," but I do sometimes want to be treated like both of those things. I never want to be punished, but I do sometimes want to experience intense sensations that don't come with that emotional baggage.

Have you ever gotten spanked and felt like you were being tended to?

Alison found every inch of my skin with a crop. Gently at first, little taps everywhere, which, if you've ever flushed with goosebumps when someone runs their fingernails down your spine, might also be for you. Then, more intense — a few quick raps, hot and bright on the meatiest part of my ass. Always with the option to bail, to say it was too much. Always, after the hardest smacks, with a simple touch, her hand to the flesh in reassurance, reminding me that I was there in my body, and she was there with me.

I surprised myself with how much intensity I could take. I do not think of myself as having a particular thirst or talent for pain. But do I feel catharsis during a tattoo? Yes. Should that have been a hint? Yes. There was something about knowing that I was in capable, careful hands that let me uncoil into this experience. The times in my life when I am not worried about tending to someone else's needs are rare, and here, with the choice to cater to someone else removed, I was given license to experience only what I was feeling in that moment. I will never, ever forget it.

After she untied me, we lay on the kitchen floor together, eating the chocolate pudding she'd made for dessert and giggling about this probably being the first time this had occurred in this particular kitchen in Harwich.

I wondered, afterward, why I'd been so unsure about diving into this experience headfirst. I realized with somewhat mortifying clarity that I've spent so much emotional energy in my life convincing my female friends that I wasn't constantly trying to fuck them, that by the time I arrived here as an adult, I wasn't sure how to go about doing the opposite. I'll be forever grateful to Alison for helping me learn this new thing about myself.

It's become a running joke with us, that I will always leave a little bit of a meal on my plate for her to finish. This is because my eyes are frequently a lot bigger than my stomach; I almost always have more enthusiasm for eating than actual physical space for it. This, now that I'm thinking of it, has become a common trope with many of my lovers, and for some reason it makes me feel very loved to be teased about it.

I love cooking for her, because she's usually hungry. She loves toast more than most anyone in history, is a vegetarian unless something exceptional is happening, and is usually willing to let me treat scalloped potatoes as a main course. I love her very much.

Of all the things I've ever cooked for her, this was one of her favorites.

Honeynut Squash Risotto with Garlic Spinach

1—2 small honeynut squash, peeled, seeded and diced
1 yellow onion, diced
2—3 Tbsp. unsalted butter
1 cup Arborio rice
1 cup white wine
1 qt. vegetable or chicken stock (look, chicken stock tastes better, but sometimes you're dating a vegetarian)
3 cloves garlic, smashed
½ bag baby spinach
Olive oil
½ a lemon
A nub of soft goat cheese
Salt and pepper, to taste

Heat the stock in a saucepan until just simmering. Keep it warm, but not bubbling.

In a wide, heavy-bottomed pot, melt most of the butter over medium heat (save a little for the spinach later), and cook the onion in it with a pinch of salt, until soft and translucent. Add the diced squash and sauté for about 5 minutes, until it's coated in butter and warmed through. Add the rice, and let it spend some time in the butter (Marcela Hazan said to cook it until the rice "becomes pregnant with butter," which I like to think about every time I make it). It will also start to turn translucent and sizzle a bit.

Once you hear it sizzle, it's time to add the wine and stir, stir, stir, until all the liquid is absorbed into the rice. Then, add one ladle of the hot stock and stir, stir, stir until it's all absorbed. Then another, and another, until you've used most of your stock — this usually takes 25 — 30 minutes depending on your rice. Taste the rice, if it still has some tooth to it, add a little more water or stock to the saucepan and get it warm quickly — the only unbreakable rule here is that once you start, you only add hot liquid to risotto rice.

Once the rice is cooked to your liking, cover the pot and turn your attention to the spinach. Give the saucepan you used for the stock a quick rinse and wipe it dry. Then, melt the rest of your butter with a glug of olive oil and the smashed garlic cloves over medium heat. Let the garlic cook in the fat until it smells good and add your spinach with a bit of salt. Sauté until the spinach wilts and turns bright green, then hit it with the juice of half a lemon and turn off the heat.

To serve, dig a little well in a bowl of risotto and pile a tangle of the sautéed spinach in there. Crumble the goat cheese over the spinach, drizzle a little olive oil over the top, and crack some black pepper over it, if you like.

Serves 2 with plenty leftover for breakfast

Provincetown: Good Men in a Storm

I've been thinking about how Provincetown has so frequently been a place to weather storms. The dune shacks served as safe havens for shipwrecked sailors. There are houses lining Commercial Street that hid people on their way to the next segment of the Underground Railroad. There have been hundreds of texts written about the comparative respite people found here during the AIDS crisis. Once I started thinking along these lines, it became impossible to miss just how many people come here after completely uprooting their lives and abandoning everything they've known to figure out who they are and how to live as that whole person.

It's goofy, but I guess I didn't realize we were doing it too.

There is, unfortunately, no way to talk about feeding the people I have loved in Provincetown without talking about quarantine.

/ QUARANTINE POD CAST OF CHARACTERS /

Me

Hi, it's me again. Only older, more dependent on alcohol for anxiety relief, more finely attuned to the man-made horrors beyond our comprehension, more concerned about the people I love remaining alive, and more eager than ever to cook for them until I'm unconscious. I think grilled cheese is a breakfast food, and I solve most moments of emotional discontent with a cheese plate.

Sean

My husband. A gentle giant — 6'4", worried, deeply obsessed with playing the right record to set the right mood in the room, for some reason reading *The Parable of the Sower* as the Coronavirus pandemic kicked into high gear. We washed our hands relentlessly on our trip home from Barbados just before lockdown began, unaware of how little that actually did to protect us and were trying to plan an all-vinyl dance party at one of our favorite basement bars in Provincetown for the following weekend, blissfully dissonant in our understanding of what the threat was and how long it would last. Sean loves tortellini en brodo so much that I promised in our wedding vows to get really good at making it. He'd already stocked our cabinet full of heirloom dried beans before the public health crisis began, because he likes to spend winter with a pot on the stove all the time, just in case we want them, or someone comes over hungry. We literally call him Bean Boy. Many of us use his height to our advantage when something is on too high a shelf, or if we need to be covered in a human-weighted blanket to block out the noise for a minute or two. He was one of the first people I realized would love me more if I was more fully myself, and that I couldn't tell him a joke that was too dark.

Kiah
Sean's then-girlfriend. Yes, yes, this is a story about a partially polyamorous quarantine pod full of mostly queer, creative weirdos, and if that's making you roll your eyes already, I recommend that you buckle up. Often described as a mermaid (by me, mostly), this blonde, tree-climbing, chicken-and-rice enthusiast was, at the time, coordinating the youth education program at the local art museum. When these quarantine dinners began, she and Sean had already

been dating for almost three years. Even still, we all had some shit to navigate through with respect to quality time spent, the division of caretaking and comforting, and how much tenderness there actually is to go around. Kiah loves horses more than most people, can be counted on to dive into any physical challenge with the enthusiasm of a Tasmanian Devil, and will play charades at the drop of a hat. When she lived in Provincetown, she spent a lot of time in the dunes — not alone, but with the companionship of her two dogs, Fox and Billie, who were such integral members of the pod that they deserve their own character blurbs. Kiah is exceptionally good at dressing herself, and somehow manages to look radiant and powerful in an art smock. She's brought the now indispensable luxury of linen sheets into my life and is responsible for teaching me an innumerable list of new things — among them block print carving and printmaking, the joy of keeping houseplants alive, where to buy the best organic seeds on the Internet, and how to sometimes say what you want without second-guessing yourself. She absolutely cannot be trusted with a box-grater.

Fox

Around nine in dog years at the time (*at least* 63 in human years), Fox is an Irish Setter / Australian Shepherd (probably) mix. His face is half white and half chestnut brown. He has a fluffy coat and looks better in a baseball hat than any human man I've ever met. Fox does not require a leash, he'll simply follow you wherever you lead him, unless you're in the dunes, in which case he'll show you the way. He's one of the gentlest dogs I've ever met, who gets anxious when you've snuggled him for too long, and hates unexpected noises. Getting him to sleep in bed with me for a whole night felt like a triumph — especially for the morning ritual of flipping onto his back and covering his nose with both paws while I scratched his belly. He'll dig a hole in the sand for as many hours as you'll let him, stopping periodically to bury his nose in the damp earth, sniffing at the mycelial network of boletes and lichen below, before hopping back up to dig again, his body rocking left to right with the joy of a labor of pure love. I have no idea why he loves to do this, but he's doing it for us, that much I'm sure of. Fox licks bowls, plates, and cooking pots clean with a methodical precision, gently stepping a white-socked foot into the pot for leverage, as he scrapes the last bits out of the corners. When he falls asleep, his tongue slips out of the front of his mouth. He is the best dog I have ever met.

Billie

Whenever I quote Billie's age, Kiah has to correct me, because I always remember her as basically a puppy. I think she was four during the time at hand. Billie is a mix of the fastest, funniest dogs in the world; she has the head of a Staffordshire Bull Terrier, the body of a Rhodesian Ridgeback, the heart of a lion, and the agility of a seal underwater. She has blown both of her ACLs out once, which Kiah spent an absolutely incredible sum of money to have fixed, because when she runs, she has no moderation. She is either still, or a bullet, flying through sand fast enough to catch up to kiteboarders, horseback riders, rabbits, the occasionally very surprised child, and if she needed to, likely a UFO. Unexpectedly, inside the house (unless she is wrestling with Fox or tearing a cardboard box into confetti-sized bits), she is one of the laziest, most affectionate dogs I have ever met. She has no personal space boundaries and is willing to be picked up and laid out across multiple members of the family, two hands never enough for the number of scratches and pets and love she demands. Billie loves cucumbers, preferring to eat them whole, tearing at them like a bone, and is forbidden from eating potatoes in any form, which make her almost immediately projectile vomit.

Daniil

My ex-boyfriend? There's a question mark there because we were always kind of dancing around the idea while we were doing it. Daniil works as a fisherman in Provincetown, mostly lobsters and scallops with the occasional bycatch that we're lucky enough to enjoy. He grew up in Belarus, went to school in Lithuania and Poland, traveled to Provincetown on a J-1 Visa, and eventually moved to New York, where he worked in a gigantic, fancy Russian restaurant, getting into all the trouble you would immediately suspect. He's a very curious person, the kind of traveler who makes friends in every airport he steps into, and always finds a way to make for himself the things most people usually buy. His dad was an engineer, and I think Daniil thinks about how his father would build something every time he does it, the pictures of which Daniil can't share with him, because we have the awful experience in common of having seen our dads die. Daniil likes a bit of whiskey in his coffee on a winter morning, considers under-cooked potatoes to be a hate crime, and will actually start a fight with you over breakfast sausage dipped in maple syrup ("DISGUSTING," he bellows, anytime it gets brought up). In our time knowing each other, we've had several successful mushroom hunts in the woods, more than one argument over what I now refer to as "breakup pasta," and innumerable, wordless sighs of reverence in each other's kitchens, about whatever is bubbling on the stove or being carefully diced into a bowl, clocking each other almost immediately as the unrepentant food perverts we both are. Daniil is about my height, which makes stealing each other's clothes pretty easy and satisfying, and he has sparkly green eyes, and a truly, truly round head. He is usually incapable of sitting still for longer than one movie, and always, *always,* shows up with a bottle of wine.

Sofia

Daniil's then-girlfriend. Sofia is from Brookline, MA, an extremely Jewish neighborhood next to Boston and comes from Jews and northern Spaniards with the legendary eyebrows and emotional baggage to prove it. She is so beautiful it's actually infuriating sometimes, despite being one of the goofiest human beings I've ever encountered. She is photogenic in a way that disorients me but is willing to send you a double-chin selfie from the toilet just to lighten your mood. She is a bizarrely talented artist, capable of rendering the most fantastical request within a matter of minutes with a pencil, and also of recreating photorealistic copies of food packaging with a brush the size of one single hair. She taught herself to do stick-and-poke tattoos by practicing on her own legs and has now permanently decorated every single one of us. She eats fruit like other people snack on potato chips and thinks a spoon of plain yogurt is one of the most disgusting things on Earth. Dude loves noodles like family and will spend hours making something no one even realized they wanted. She says things like, "I'm going to watch the sunset every day for the rest of the year," and then actually goes on to almost do it. I envy her energy and enthusiasm, and I also worry about her. I want to protect her from the world, from herself, from the burnout. She and Daniil met, of course, in an airport, which is so entirely befitting of the way they both move through the world. When the pandemic started, Sofia was living in Brookline with her parents. After a long walk between two oceanside beaches in Wellfleet where Daniil stopped several times to call her on the phone, he'd managed to convince her to move to Provincetown and work at our restaurant. An arrangement of which I was — I think understandably — suspicious. But once I met Sofia, I knew how special she was. In this instance, Daniil was right.

Alison

My then-girlfriend. In reality, "girlfriend" isn't really the adequate word for the casual, lovely, enduring-from-a-distance, romantic friendship we have shared. You already met this person, you know a lot about her kitchen, but you should know more about her. I met Alison because Sean sent her Tinder profile to me with a nudge, "Hot, right?" He'll be eternally proud of that, and he deserves to be, because our connection has been profound, and we've learned a lot from each other. Also, because he was right, she is incredibly hot — long-limbed, elegant, with a beautiful smile and an absolutely gravity-defying ass. When we first started dating, she was between grad school stints. She eventually decided to finish her master's in landscape architecture at

Harvard, in her hometown of Cambridge — a fact she rolled her eyes about when she finally decided. She is, as that might indicate, brilliant. During the initial quarantine period of the COVID-19 pandemic, Harvard, like most other universities, went remote, which meant Alison was free to rent a little cottage in Wellfleet and join our pod. It was during this period that I learned even more about her than I already knew. She is obsessed with marking the changing of the seasons with Solstice / Equinox feasts. She absolutely refuses to waste leftovers. She treats shrimp cocktail like an ultimate luxury. She keeps food scraps for compost in her freezer. She makes incredible applesauce, apple cake, and puts heavy cream in her coffee. She has just taught herself to finally enjoy the texture of mushrooms, always wants just a little something for dessert, and introduced us all to the genius that is Bryant Terry, which we were especially grateful for, because it helped us feed Tess better.

Tess

Ben's girlfriend. There are a lot of ways you could describe Tess to someone who's never met her. She's an unbelievably gifted artist, whose hyper-detailed line drawings of the flora of the dunes regularly leave me speechless. She's a gifted landscape designer, whose slight frame very much belies just how far she can drag her entire weight in soil and dried leaves. She's extremely soft-spoken, which makes her willful stubbornness even more surprising when you first encounter it. Tess was raised by vegan Vermont hippies and has been carrying on in their tradition ever since. While it's often challenging to manage these restrictions alongside the generally hedonistic diets the rest of us keep, it's also taught me a lot about developing flavors and creating richness without animal fat. I can, as it turns out, make a pretty banging vegan gravy, a thing I absolutely wouldn't have tried if it weren't for Thanksgiving with Tess. I've seen this woman fuck up a cake so hard I would join the witness protection program, and she just dives right back in and tries again, joking about how bad the last one was. She and Ben make their own kombucha, sprout their own tempeh, inoculate their own mushroom logs, and keep a formidable garden that's supplied us all with our weight in cucumbers. She's also extremely competitive, which makes her a joy to play dice with.

Ben
Tess's boyfriend. He probably doesn't know this, but I always describe him to other people as a Labrador — he comes off as sweet, genuine, dopey, and a lot of fun to act stupid with, and then his innate intelligence blasts through the conversation at the least expected time and blows everyone's minds. Ben grew up in central Pennsylvania, so he has a hankering for pickled bologna, hard pretzels, and knows more about Three Mile Island than anyone else. After a brief stint as a concrete safety testing expert (*what?*), Ben traveled the world working in ski lodges, restaurants, and bars, fine-tuning his bartending and people-managing skills. He can have a conversation with absolutely anyone, and often arrives at our house with a Yeti cooler full of painkiller or margarita makings. He is a gear-obsessed person — he and Kiah have been joking for years about starting a podcast called "Gearz and Beerz" where they just talk about their bikes and tents and what headlamp is best — and considers 20 miles to be a "short bike

ride." Ben knows more about mushrooms than anyone I know, and he takes better pictures than almost all of them too. He loves puns more than any human being, and brings levity, laughter, and incredibly weird facts to every dinner table with him. He loves kitesurfing, their cat Sasha, and raising garden worms. Krampus night (December 6) is his favorite holiday.

/ THE SETTING: PROVINCETOWN /

MARCH — JUNE 2020

DURING THE FIRST WAVE OF THE COVID-19 PANDEMIC

We knew we were getting away with something other people couldn't. We knew that a six to eight person quarantine pod blurred the lines of responsibility. Most of us weren't working at this point, it being March on Cape Cod. Those of us who were, were doing it remotely, or on a boat, or in gardens. We communicated transparently about our activities outside each other's homes. We split grocery store runs, taking turns gathering everyone else's lists. We went to the liquor store as infrequently as possible. We wore masks, latex gloves, sanitized our hands before and after, followed the arrows painted on the floor of the grocery store aisles, and tried not to touch our phones or faces. Some of it, of course, was overkill. Some of it, we would learn, was totally misguided. But we did the best we could, because we wanted to feed each other, and because more than anything, we wanted to be together.

We have access to so many wonderful elements of culture in Provincetown, but one thing we definitely don't have is a diverse food culture. That forced us to be resourceful and willing to experiment in ways that we maybe wouldn't have before. We couldn't go to Chinatown for dim sum, so Sofia and I tried to do it ourselves. We couldn't go out for Indian food, so I learned to make homemade naan. We couldn't take a road trip through the South, so Sean ordered me an entire leg of Benton's aged ham. We, obviously, didn't have a ham stand, so Daniil made one out of an old cutting board and driftwood (I know). Kiah wanted schnitzel for her birthday, so I made schnitzel. Sean wanted to make gumbo for his, so we got andouille and Tasso ham in the mail from Louisiana.

Birthdays were a consistent challenge. Mine was the first one, halfway through April, when we hoped this might all end in a month or two. I had a new lover that I wanted to invite, but because he wasn't part of the pod, I didn't. This was before Alison, Ben, and Tess had joined us, so the plan was that Kiah, Sean, Daniil, Sofia, and I were going to cut a channel down the length of that Benton's ham and take shots of bourbon from it until we fell asleep — a ham luge. Something I can't take credit for. This was Sean Brock's idea: I'd heard him talk about it on television years before his eventual sobriety (his version involved Pappy Van Winkle, because *obviously*), and had always wanted to do it for a birthday. It was excessive, insanely indulgent, kind of gross, and definitely not the most COVID-safe birthday plan. But during a moment in history when we weren't sure we'd ever get to do stupid, gross, indulgent things again, it seemed like the right moment to seize.

Then, what we were all hoping wouldn't happen did happen: One of the guys Daniil worked with on the boat woke up with a sore throat and a fever. Daniil and Sofia both felt fine, but as this was our first real brush with known exposure, they ducked out of the pod for 14 days, then, the prevailing recommendation, just to be sure. This blew up the birthday plan pretty solidly, turning what was a small party into a ham luge for three. Sean and Kiah rallied spectacularly, collecting oysters from across the street to roast with herb butter, buying enough champagne to actually drown us all, dressing up for a party like they really meant it. Their efforts were kicked into high gear by Flynn doing what she does best — spoiling us from a distance. She sent a Russ & Daughters care package of bagels, cream cheese, lox, caviar, blini, and pickles that truly saved the day. Other friends absolutely crushed the curbside-care-package-drop-off routine that we would all get terribly good at over the ensuing year. Sofia especially making her mark with a line drawing of the feast table of our future, and a gigantic chunk of Parmesan — the thing I had forgotten to get during the last bi-weekly grocery store journey, and had actually cried over, the membrane between not crying and crying being absolutely paper-thin in those early days.

Each birthday after that — Sofia's in July, Ben's in August, Alison's in September, Kiah's in December, Sean's and Daniil's in January, mine and Tess's again in April (we were absolutely *shocked* to still be celebrating these in quarantine) — all seemed to come with the mandated disappearance of one or more members of the gang due to a brush with the virus. We got better at them, more creative with what we could accomplish on the porch, more aware of asymptomatic windows and risk factors than we ever thought we would have to be. This curse extended all the way through to August 2022, when I got COVID for the first time, a day before Ben's birthday. I texted our group chat (which I titled QUARANTINECULE 2020 — naively thinking that would be the only year we needed it):

Me: "My brain just now: "Oh, it's Ben's birthday tomorrow, so one of us had to get it."

Kiah: "Covid: ruining the pod's birthdays since 2020."

Sean: "Classic."

Tess: "The chaos <a cake, of course> I'm about to try to transport to the Beer Garden — I wish you could all be there to eat it with us! It might taste good!"

This bizarre period of extreme intimacy we all experienced together had made us even closer than we would have been otherwise. There's a platonic shorthand now — we remember how Kiah plays "Stump," which, for the uninitiated, consists of standing in a circle, tossing a hammer in the air, and trying to catch it by the handle in order to whack a nail into a tree stump — what could possibly go wrong? We know the moment Sean will start making us watch YouTube videos until the wee hours of the morning. We remember the time Alison's cat James visited her litter box during the middle of dinner and we all thought one of us had absolutely *ripped ass* at the table. We remember Sofia's triumphant blackjack win on New Year's Eve with the weird set of chocolate poker chips someone's relative gave us. "It's just chocolate!" she screamed each time she cleaned us out. We know that you can't sit Ben and Sean next to each other when you play Telestrations, because their drawings are unhinged in exactly the same way and throw the entire game into chaos. We know that Daniil will eat absolutely anything that's on the counter next to whatever is *actually* for dinner. We know that Tess will play Zonk in the most conservative way possible, until we realize she's beating all of us. I don't know what they think about me while they chuckle to themselves — maybe I'll find out in one of their memoirs someday.

We were scared and unsure of what the future held, but we were rarely bored and almost always full. This, of course, is a story of privilege. We were lucky and nourished, and very far away from our former lives stacked on top of strangers in cities, untouched by the grief that visited so many others. We were hiding together at the end of the world, none of us by accident, and we were so lucky to reap the benefits of each other's talents and idiosyncrasies. There is absolutely no one else I'd rather live through the end of the world with. Good men in a storm.

Provincetown: Acidity Is a Feeling

This is stupid, but there was a point at which I thought I just wouldn't ever get COVID. We'd been surgically careful at the beginning of the pandemic and took a lot longer to get back to "normal" than most people. Our caution lost us friendships, business opportunities, beach raves, memories. But it was all worth it, we thought, to keep each other safe.

Once we were all vaccinated and boosted, a few of us got sick and came out on the other side mostly unscathed. At a certain point, it felt crazy to be the only one wearing a KN95 at a drag show, to be the only one asking for an outside table in the rain, to be the only one testing before a dinner party. So, at a certain point, we just stopped. We went to the Old Colony Tap. We hosted a weekly dance party. We met our friends at bars with no airflow. And then, as if science could have predicted it, I tested positive the Saturday of Carnival Week. If you've never experienced Carnival in Provincetown, just imagine a lower budget Mardi Gras with way more chest harnesses and more people than the sewer system can gracefully handle. It also happens to be the second-busiest week of our year at Pop+Dutch, the little sandwich shop at the center of our lives.

I was really careful before July 4th week. I was really careful before Bear Week. And then, to be honest, I kind of thought we were in the clear. I'm writing now from my bed, on day five of testing positive. My fever has receded, my sense of taste has disappeared, I still have this strange knot of congestion in an inaccessible recess behind my sinuses, and going up and down the stairs more than once gets me winded. I feel so lucky to be vaccinated and boosted, and so utterly abandoned by the medical and legislative communities.

A week before I tested positive, the CDC amended its guidance to say that after five days of quarantine, even if you are still testing positive, you can go back out into the world, masked. I'm not an epidemiologist, but to me, the science behind that doesn't seem to — well — exist.

My symptoms started on a Friday with an itchy throat, sneezing, gross congestion. I'd had a cold a few weeks before, so I assumed I'd cooked myself up a sinus infection and tried to get an appointment at our overrun, beleaguered health clinic. Monday, after work was the best I could do. I took it, hoping I wouldn't need it. That night (this is a familiar refrain by now) I woke up with chills, a fever, brutal muscle aches, and the kind of headache we usually pathologize. The next day, I dragged myself to urgent care, still certain it was a sinus infection because I'd rapid tested myself so many times. After a long wait outside, a nurse handed me a nasal swab to perform on myself, now almost second nature. I sat in the car, with the windows rolled down to await my results, trying to take box breaths and make sure nothing was going crazy at Pop+Dutch in my absence. The phone rang, the nurse from inside on the other end.

"Hi honey, I just want to let you know that you've tested very positive for Covid. You need to go home and rest, stay inside and away from other people for five days. After five days, if you still test positive, you can go out wearing a mask. Do you have any questions?"

So now, I'm lying in my bed, with a box of tissues next to me in case I sneeze *productively,* taking 1,000 mg of acetaminophen every six hours to keep my head from exploding, trying desperately to taste anything, and thinking about how tomorrow, Carnival Day, I will feel pressure from my staff, my partner, the CDC, and — most severely — myself to go in to work at my restaurant wearing two masks, and desperately praying I don't get anyone sick, on one of the busiest, most chaotic days of the year.

If I wake up and test negative, I'll go. My stamina will, no doubt, be reduced. My productivity will, no doubt, be decimated. My brain will, no doubt, not be firing on all cylinders. At the end of the day, rather than hang out on the stoop drinking margaritas with the crew and watching the parade, I will try to slip out of the building and back to my bed before the thousands of costumed revelers swirl around me — still aching and coughing — in the street. If I wake up and test positive again, I will stay home, feeling guilty for not being able to help, and salty for missing the soul-bonding experience of sitting on the stoop drinking margaritas.

Sean and the crew at Pop+Dutch have held things down remarkably well in my absence. I've tried to help any way I can from here — writing the schedule, ordering the mayonnaise, trying to estimate how many cases of eggs and chicken they went through while I wasn't there. But that does nothing to alleviate the fatigue of everyone trying to make up for the manual labor that I do next to them every day. The big rounds of dishes, the carrying of the 50 pound sack of flour up the stairs, the crouching down to drain and refill the steam oven. Never mind the mental and emotional labor — the scheduling questions, the ingredient questions, the "where does this go?" everyday dance that we all usually do together.

To keep him virus-free and our livelihood functioning, Sean and I have been masking in the house. I stay upstairs in the bedroom, he has the downstairs kitchen and living room, where he's slept on the pull-out couch for a week. We share a bathroom, where we both wear a mask unless we absolutely have to take it off to brush our teeth or shower. It's important to note that we're extremely lucky – if Sean got sick at the same time and we had to shut the whole operation down, we'd be upset, but it probably wouldn't ruin us. But I wouldn't say that on behalf of anyone of our staff having to miss a full week of wages and tips. Where would that leave them? Lots of people in Provincetown make their money for the entire year during the summer, so missing a full, busy week like this one might be the equivalent to a month at your year-round job. All this on the tail end of one of the busiest, most challenging, and most personally heartbreaking summer seasons we've ever had.

This is careful choreography that millions of people have had to figure out on their own, to varying degrees of success. I feel so lucky to have been able to wait this long to learn the steps, and for my symptoms and our circumstances to have not been more severe.

Even so, we are, to be honest, barely holding it together. Everyone's nerves are frazzled, bodies exhausted, the moments between crying and not crying very brief. This, to be fair, is always true in August, but did any of us really need to be living through this without an ounce of official support? There is no more Covid leave assistance, no more free rapid Covid testing, no more Covid relief grants. But clearly ... there is still Covid, right? We may not need to live in fear of death or hospitalization, but it is still capable of wreaking havoc on our lives, right?

The two selfish, petty things I want the most right now are: 1) a really big hug, and 2) to be able to taste a double cheeseburger.

My sense of taste disappeared sometime between Saturday and Sunday, and because I am the way that I am, I've been doing experiments with what flavors and scents are strong enough to break through. So far, not many.

The first real one came Monday — I made myself a bowl of the spiciest, saltiest, cheapest ramen possible. I did my usual tricks of stirring in sesame oil, rice vinegar, soy, and chili crisp. Because I hadn't eaten a vegetable in a few days, I tossed in a handful of baby spinach, and a small bowl of the yellow cherry tomatoes I harvested from the garden. I fizzed up some Emergen-C powder in a tumbler of water, and took it all outside to the back porch, to get my allotted 15 minutes of sunshine and fresh air for the day. The ramen was... hot. I could tell that it was salty, but I wouldn't say that I could really taste that. The spice from the chili sizzled on my tongue, but also without any real flavor. This is a very disorienting experience. Then, I popped a broth-warmed cherry tomato in my mouth and realized something very important: *tomatoes feel like something.* The acidity — which really is more of a feeling than a flavor, I realized — washed over my tongue, mixed with the other sensations, and it was the closest I've been to *tasting* in many days.

I grew these heirloom tomato plants from teeny tiny seeds that arrived in the mail in teeny tiny plastic bags set inside teeny tiny envelopes. They sprouted on a bench next to our dining table this winter, got re-potted and set on the deck in the spring, then finally buried deep in compost in the garden in the summer. I inspected them every day, checking for pests, pinching off suckers, watering them gently at the base of their stems. I snipped branches off the privets and lilacs to give them more sunshine and set up trellises once their lush branches outgrew their cages. We've spent this whole year together so far, and they really came through for me this August, in a way I didn't expect to need them to.

It's really easy to be lonely and find despair while you're sick. But tomatoes feel like something.

New Orleans: I Missed You Both So Much at Lunch

I have always been prone to crushes. I swoon in and out of love easily and quickly, and I'm never quite sure where and for what it's going to hit. I say "what" because it's not just people, it's also places – cities, lookout points, and most especially, restaurants. My crush on Galatoire's in New Orleans began on Sean's and my first visit there in 2014. We were in the process of opening our sandwich shop, I was about to turn 30, and we were both exhausted, frazzled, and excited. When Sean announced that he thought we should finally go to New Orleans for a last hurrah before work began, I didn't argue. I was, as ever, ready for a Sazerac.

Our last visit to New Orleans before Covid started was in April of 2019. Isn't it funny how many things we have to qualify with that thought now, in the after times? Aren't we lucky to have mostly just missed restaurants and lookout points and cities, and not had to mourn for loved one after loved one like lots of other folks?

On this trip in 2019, we had no idea what was to come, of course. Only that we were about to open the shop for another season, that our friend was turning 40 and wanted to get silly, and that I really wanted to have a fancy lunch before it all went down. Being in New Orleans has always put me in an immediately romantic mood, and as I wrestled heartburn back down into my belly that afternoon, I wrote this letter to Daniil and Dori, both of whom I missed very much at lunch.

APRIL 18, 2019 — 4:29 PM

Dearest Darlings,

Our waiter's nametag said "Evangelista." I wanted to ask whether it was a first, last or nickname, but the silver streaks in his long, slicked-back hair and his clear, modern-framed glasses atop his 6'5" tuxedoed frame kept me quiet and polite.

I ordered a 2005 Bourgogne Aligoté — a wine I have never had but have tasted in my brain. A buttery, minerally, Sancerre cousin made of old world techniques by loving nerds' hands, I knew it was what I wanted to drink with lunch before I tasted it. Evangelista brought glasses and an ice bucket ten minutes later and said, "they're digging for your selection." It was hard not to feel like M.F.K. Fisher, waiting for an ancient bottle of Marc to drink with her trout almondine.

Galatoire's is one of the only places I've ever loved whose default table setting includes a fish fork. We started with oysters Rockefeller — allegedly containing over 20 ingredients between the aromatics, the binder, the absinthe, and the thick, fat gulf oyster that serves as its bedrock. Today, they charred them extra hard, so the usually verdant green tops were pitch black, and the just-barely-cooked oyster underneath was steaming hot, bursting with brine, and mingled with the butter and herbs perched atop it uncommonly well.

Then there were the soufflé potatoes — fried three times, in three oil baths, at three different temperatures, until a simple plank of potato puffs up into a hollow boat, meant to ferry as much béarnaise sauce into your mouth at once as possible.

The Aligoté cut through all the richness it was meant to and cleared space for the indulgences to come. We'd each come with preconceived ideas of what our birthday lunch entrees would be — Shrimp Creole for Sean and Crab Sardou for me. But then Evangelista did exactly what the fuck a tuxedoed waiter is meant to do and blew up our plans.

"I do just want you to know that there are crawfish tails and soft-shelled crabs today, prepared as you prefer them, of course."

Sean jumped immediately at crawfish étouffée with white rice (a traditionalist to the end), and I negotiated with Evangelista until a sautéed soft-shelled crab appeared, bathed in brown butter with a single lemon wedge and a side of creamed spinach. The compulsory Tabasco sauce on the table was the period at the end of that particular sentence.

While the bacchanalia at our table unfolded, two "old-timers" sat down at the table next to us. They shook hands with every single waiter. "Hello, Doc. Hello, Brian," they each exalted. Doc and Brian received a plate of garlic bread instead of the usual French loaf, two gin and tonics with a plate of lemons, olives, and pickled onions ("salad,"

Evangelista explained — swoon), and a combo plate of shrimp remoulade and crab Maison — all without asking for them.

I have decided that whatever sins Doc and Brian have committed to get to this point (and judging by their lavender bowties and slate gray pinstripe suits, they are chilling and many), they've done something right in their lives to get treated this way in this green and gold hall of earthly delights.

I missed you both so much at lunch.

Yours,
Rebecca

I don't know if it was how much M.F.K. Fisher I'd been reading at the time, or some writerly "presentiment of loss," as Joan Didion put it, but I felt freakishly compelled to commit this experience to memory, to immortalize it by sharing it with the people I love, even if it only ever lived in my Notes app like I expected it would.

The day after this lunch, we saw our waiter, Evangelista, bopping down the street along with us in the same second line uptown. He was wearing jeans and a tie-dyed shirt, huge sunglasses, unquestionably stoned out of his mind, dancing down the street with the abandon of a man who has shed his work tuxedo. He passed away in 2020, which I found out through mutual friends in New Orleans. He was, of course, a beloved figure in the city, having waited tables at Galatoire's for nearly 15 years, and having immersed himself in second-line culture with the Krewe Du Vieux. I came across an interview he did with Gabe Borges for the Loyola Department of History, talking about his time in the service industry and his love for the weirdness of Galatoire's and the city at large.

"I hear a horn and I'm like 'where is it?' And uh you know, Galatoire's is a weird intersection of that, because we have a brass band in front of us all the time and if it's a really over the top Friday lunch you have a second line band just come off the street and work their way around the room, cause somebody wanted them to come in. It's yea, a weird intersection of magic. It does like, it's part of what doesn't make sense if you're an outsider sitting there, trying to enjoy what you thought was a certain type of meal, but then every customer in the restaurant who does get what's going on has gotten up and is following the band around the room ya know, and sorry they bumped your table, but you just, the culture just engulfed you completely, ya know. Live it. It doesn't happen every day."

I never got to know Chris Evangelista personally, but I can tell you that next time I'm there, I will miss him very much at lunch.

II.

Rio Rancho: How to Live Through a Huge Mistake

I was a strange four-year-old. My favorite toy was my Fisher-Price kitchen playset, I was more interested in books than trampolines, and I always, always preferred olives and cheese to candy and cakes. There was one exception to this rule, of course: frosting.

I was the kid (and occasionally am still the adult) who would eat the buttercream roses left behind on other peoples' plates, even (and sometimes especially) the cheap supermarket cakes with the frosting that crunches a little bit because it contains more sugar than it can chemically absorb. The fact that this substance is mostly butter has clarified this position for me in my adulthood and helped me understand why I'd eat the frosting off a cupcake and leave the cake part behind, and why my mouth would water when I saw one of those stupid little cardboard tubs of Duncan-Hines vanilla frosting in the refrigerator.

I was also extremely little. I had the kind of pediatric visits up through adolescence where the doctors would insist that my parents feed me a milkshake for breakfast before school, so that I'd land in the proper weight class for my age (a solution I thought was disgusting then and think is disgusting now).

"You just have his metabolism," my mother would remind me afterward, gesturing to my father's 6'3", 180 pound frame, or what you might think of when you hear the word "beanpole."

"Enjoy it while it lasts."

I don't remember myself as being particularly sneaky, or that I had any reason to be. But I was an only child until my brother was born when I was seven, so I had lots of time on my own to be quietly curious in all the different rooms of our little house in Rio Rancho, New Mexico.

I steered clear of the bathrooms – I'd already come upon more centipedes and scorpions there than I needed for the rest of my life. Growing up in the desert is strange in ways you cannot imagine.

I discovered the surprisingly comprehensive stash of *Playboy* magazines on a bookshelf in the living room one day and leafed through them with open-mouthed reverence. We weren't conservative about having bodies and being human beings, but we also weren't an extremely naked family. By this time in my life, I'd seen my father naked maybe once, my mother naked more times than I could count, and I'd already stared at all the parts of my body I could get up to a mirror. But these were strangers! Their boobs were so round, and there was so much make-up, and so much less pubic hair than I would have expected. I was entranced, and would sneak a visit to each month's issue, chronologically, whenever I was left briefly to my own devices. But once one or both of my parents noticed that these magazines had been moved around, leafed through, put back out of order, they were suddenly moved to a shelf much too high for me to grasp.

Once, I opened a jewelry box on my mother's night table and found a stash of condoms. Having absolutely no idea what I was looking at, I squished one of the packages around in my fingers and tried to understand the words on the label. If we're being honest, I probably thought this was some forbidden food I'd never been allowed to try. I asked my mom what they were, and she, uncharacteristically prudish, shut the box and simply said, "None of your concern." I was asking her this question while perched on their California king waterbed, in front of floor-to-ceiling mirrors in their bedroom.

Since my bedroom and my playroom were basically the spaces I knew best in the world, this left the kitchen for solo expeditions. I was extremely curious to taste things in the refrigerator or cupboard, and the thing I was most consistently reprimanded for (until the joint pleasures of alcohol and making out were introduced to me much later) was standing in front of the refrigerator with the door open while I did so.

Somehow, even my teeny tiny curious brain began to understand that there are things that you just can't do in front of other people. You can't look at magazines with boobs in them, you can't eat the condoms in your parents' nightstand, and you most certainly can't stick your finger into the Duncan-Hines vanilla frosting tub and eat it with the refrigerator door open. And so, I waited.

The few times I was most reliably left alone in those days were when my dad was at work and my mom was in the shower. I learned, like all little weirdos do, to savor that unobserved time. It was usually just a snack and a book at the kitchen table, and for little weirdos like me, that was often enough. But occasionally I ... well, I acted like a little sneak. Once the *Playboys* had been foisted into the heavens, my attention turned to the fridge and the pantry (blessedly, before I'd really considered trying to eat the condoms). One day, I noticed a huge tub of frosting, as yet un-opened in the pantry. It was at least twice as big as any tub of frosting I'd ever seen in the fridge, and I felt like I'd discovered sweet, sweet El Dorado.

My mother, who gave me the best kind of attention a four-year-old could ask for had probably made me one of my favorite things to eat — sometimes half an avocado stuffed with chicken salad like a boat, with a little sail of cheddar cheese, or a plate full of raw vegetables cut into flower shapes to look like a garden (legitimately something she made for me once, with no idea how regularly I would ask for it again). She went off to shower, hopefully without having to kill a scorpion, and I made what remains one of the worst mistakes of my life.

I wedged my little body on a bottom shelf of the slender pantry and closed the door behind me, the enormous tub of vanilla frosting in my hands. I peeled the plastic lid off to reveal the foil shield. I was too young to understand that piercing this barrier meant the contents would need to go into the refrigerator and would immediately give away my unsophisticated espionage. And so, I peeled that slim foil barrier all the way off, and stuck not just my finger, but my whole greedy little hand into the smooth, cool, white goop, and put as much of it as I could fit into my mouth.

There have been times in my life when my punishment for poor judgment has been as unpleasant, but rarely as swift, since this was not, in fact, a tub of vanilla frosting, but rather Crisco.

At first, I was simply confused. Why ... wasn't it sweet? Why ... wasn't it melting on my tongue? Why ... wasn't this delicious? Why ... was I gagging? I didn't know what Crisco was then, I only knew that I had to get it out of my mouth immediately. I kicked the pantry door open, spit the ping-pong ball-sized mound of shortening directly into the trash can, and sank into one further level of despair when I realized that whatever this was still coated my tongue and the roof of my mouth.

I grabbed a sheet of paper towel and desperately *wiped my tongue with it.* I folded it in half and did it again. I drank cold water (worse). I let warm water from the faucet run directly over my tongue like a dog at a hose. It was still there, but it wasn't as bad, and I had just heard the shower turn off in my parents' bathroom. I did my best to clean up my mess (although I'm sure I left the open tub of Crisco in the pantry and never heard a word about it afterward) and sat back down at the table, staring blindly at my book, wizened and grizzled by the hard lesson I'd just scooped onto my own tongue.

I have no memory of what happened after my mother got out of the shower that day. I didn't tell anyone about this until I was well into my 20s. Looking back on this, I don't think I've ever seen my mother use Crisco for anything and have no idea why it was even in the cabinet for me to discover. To this day, thinking about it makes me put my head into my hands and retain a mild urge to gag. And I've never again stuck my finger into a frosting container.

If there are any lessons to be learned from this experience (other than, like, how to read a fucking label), it's that you have to be prepared for the kind of immediate trouble that lust can get you into, and that you can usually live through even the worst mistakes you'll ever make.

Rio Rancho: Who Taught Me How

We ate a lot of frozen vegetables when I was a kid. That's not a criticism.

My parents met in a bar in Syracuse, New York, where they were both in college. As the legend goes, Sue was standing on a table, with a pitcher of beer in each hand, challenging anyone in the bar to a drinking contest. Marc, as the legend goes, said to his friend, "I think I'd like to meet that woman."

There are lots of legends like these about my parents. There's the one about the time a guy in a billiard hall tried to get my mom's attention by grabbing her by the waist: He ripped a belt loop on her favorite pair of denim bellbottoms, and she shoved him backwards over a pool table. There's the one about the time a cat bit my dad, so he bit it back. The incongruity of both of their personalities with these stories has always struck me. My dad was a calm, rational, level-headed nerd who hardly ever drank, explaining that he liked to be "in control of all of his faculties," and would go out of his way to help anyone who needed him. My mom is a sweet, sensitive, creative person, who wants affection, validation, and camaraderie more than anything else in the world. But these were their college days, their wild times, the times of psychedelics and Grateful Dead concerts, the times before my mom gave birth to me when she was only 24 and he was only 26, when they strapped my car seat to the middle console of their white MG convertible and drove me home from the hospital.

I think a lot about them at that age, having decided to make a life on Quixote Drive in Rio Rancho, New Mexico, in a brand-new housing development that scraped at the edge of the unconquered desert. Their three-bedroom, two-bathroom home that they bought for $60,000 in 1983 seemed so tiny to me for so long, and now seems like as much as I'd ever need. It was a corner property with a huge back yard, a steep, narrow driveway, and a tiny little porch up front that we never, ever sat on. My mom planted hollyhocks and grape hyacinth in the front entryway, which barely survived the arid summers. We grew strawberries and yellow, pear-shaped tomatoes in the backyard, where there was a sour cherry tree that I miss every single day of my life. One of my earliest ambitions was to beat the birds to the cherries on the higher branches, but both the young tree's limbs and my own were too spindly to climb it. Even still, I managed to fill buckets with sour cherries, giving myself stomachache after stomachache, by eating the whole bucket and seeing how far into the street I could spit the pits.

I think about them deciding at that age that they wanted to have kids, and that they were ready to do it. Just prior to this big decision, they were both working at an ad agency in Albuquerque, making art and new friends, and probably still occasionally tripping their balls off in the desert, throwing their huge Halloween parties in the tiny casita they lived in near the university campus.

It's occurred to me that they came to this decision when my mom was the same age I was when my dad died, and I wonder often what all of our lives would look like now if he hadn't.

Cultural attitudes about how old we should be when we raise kids have been shifting ever-forward, but it's hard for me to imagine anyone I know having had kids before they were 30. I, incredibly, remember the surprise 30th birthday party my mom threw for my dad. There was a band in the backyard of a friend's house, with a huge potluck on folding tables, and my mom wore a peach and white sundress with flowers on it that I wanted as my own.

My parents always had what felt like hundreds of friends around — usually fellow artists or Deadheads or both. I liked some of them better than others. One of my favorites, Bill Archer, sometimes appeared on the doorstep without warning, having just hitchhiked up from Mexico or Peru or somewhere, with silver bracelets for me and stories of alien abductions in the desert. Mary and Mike McDade were our sweet neighbors across the backyard fence — their yard was full of different species of cacti, and just beyond that treacherous expanse they had a sunroom with huge papasan chairs that you had to race the drunk adults to get into. When they had parties at their house, there was always a relish plate with sweet and sour pickles, green and black olives, and usually a crockpot full of meatballs, and a cooler full of ice and canned Shasta in every flavor. Sometimes, I'd ride the stationary bike in their guest room during parties so that I wouldn't have to talk to anyone.

I remember my mom's 30th birthday, too — hers was celebrated at a Halloween party they threw once a year called The Annual Altered States Bash. Once a year, my mom dragged the hand-painted cardboard panels out of the garage that made the whole house look like a dungeon in a castle. She employed me to hang lights shaped like ghosts and bats, to weave fake spiderwebs through the bookshelves, and to fill the front yard with Styrofoam headstones and plastic bones (she still does this to this day, albeit without the cardboard dungeon walls and without me and my brother as helpers). On this particular Halloween, the year my mom and I both dressed up as mermaids, complete with tails she made us by hand, a party guest in a gorilla mask showed up alone, and no one could figure out who he was. At the end of the night, he ripped off the mask to reveal that he was my mom's middle brother Jamie, who'd surprised her by flying in from New York, and she screamed "OH MY GOD, IT'S MY BROTHER!" while everyone cheered and danced around them.

"He knew which drawer the silverware was in, so I knew he was someone we knew," my mom explained to me later.

My children will remember no such parties. They will likely never exist. It's a decision I feel uncertain about at almost all times, except when wars and wildfires break out, when "saying gay" and accessing abortion gets banned, when I wake up in the middle of the night afraid that Sean isn't breathing for absolutely no reason whatsoever.

This is a digression from the point at hand, which is that my parents, as tiny little baby people in their mid 20s, managed to feed me two or three square meals a day.

My dad made me a grilled cheese sandwich every morning for breakfast, since I pretty much ignored all other breakfast foods until I was old enough to drink at brunch. There were two versions of this, depending on the pace of our morning and how early I'd been able to drag my unwilling little body out of bed. He was the only morning person in our family, so in the mornings it was usually just the two of us. The most frequent grilled cheese was quick and dirty — two pieces of toast in the toaster, American cheese in between, tossed in the microwave until the cheese melted, cut into four squares. I tolerated this grilled cheese, but it was not the grilled cheese I loved.

The second, and far superior version, happened on weekend mornings, or as a reward for getting up on time and finishing my homework with him at the table while he read the newspaper. This grilled cheese was browned in butter in a frying pan on the stove, with Muenster cheese — enough Muenster cheese that it would ooze out the sides and make a cat's cradle of cheese bridges when I bit into it — cut diagonally into two triangles (I have no idea why he decided to cut each of them in different shapes, but the superiority of the sandwich triangle cannot be denied). On these mornings, his breakfast would be the orange-rind heel of this salty, squeaky, ersatz product of American exceptionalism, and a seemingly endless cup of coffee. Cheese for breakfast made sense to me. Coffee would take longer for me to figure out.

As opposed to breakfast, at dinner, the line between what was every day and what was a special occasion became decidedly blurred. There were steamed whole artichokes with melted butter, like, once a week. The broiler popped and sizzled with lamb chops and cheeseburgers. Once every few months, there was hot oil fondue, with small plates of raw meat and vegetables, and dipping sauces that we'd stir together ourselves in little ramekins — my dad would always curse while struggling to light the Sterno can, and I would always spear the tip of my finger with a fondue fork, but we persevered and ate like kings. At least once a month, we'd eat a full New England boiled dinner — corned beef, cabbage, carrots, onions, potatoes. My mom simmered tiny Cornish hens in "Master Sauce" — a certainly bastardized take on a Cantonese aromatic soy sauce-based stock that you freeze and reuse over and over again, building layers of fats and flavors from the meat that gets braised in it. There was almost always meat on the table, this being the late 80s, almost unfailingly with a starch and a vegetable.

As anyone who has ever been responsible for keeping a family fed can tell you, this is a fuckload of labor. And this is where frozen vegetables came in. Frozen green beans, frozen broccoli, frozen spinach — all with butter and salt, cooked in the microwave. On the rare occasions that dinner was just my dad and me, there were frozen lima beans or brussels sprouts, two things we both loved that my mom physically recoiled at the sight of. Sometimes there was frozen corn. I grew to love frozen peas with pearl onions. For a while there was this crazy medley of rotini pasta, crinkle-cut carrot coins, and broccoli (Frozen pasta? Who was in charge at Bird's Eye in 1989?!). Once, there was a frozen hashbrown casserole with broccoli and cheese that I have never ever seen again, and still, on occasion, desperately scan the freezer aisle for.

I knew that we weren't eating like most of the kids I went to school with. Anytime my friends would come for dinner, their eyes would get a little wide. I think most of them ate their first artichoke at our house. I also knew that we didn't have a lot of money. We bought steak when it was on sale, we ate out infrequently — I could tell that my parents were spending money on food in a very purposeful way, because they loved it, and they wanted me to love it too.

Their creativity and their kindness blow me away, looking back on this as an adult. Knowing what I know now about how easy it is to transfer your own anxieties and trauma onto your kids, to ensure your baggage will be replicated and carried around with someone else, to be unintentionally cruel — I'm just in awe, honestly, of how good a job they did. I know that's not the juiciest thing to say about your parents, but they were teaching me to be curious, grateful, open-minded, well-nourished, generous, and creative at an age where I was playing beer pong, blowing up my whole life, moving across the country. I'm so proud of them.

I was so lucky, and when my brother came along in 1991, he was lucky too. I loved shopping for baby food, thinking about what flavor Jason would next get to try for the first time. I thought it was fun to watch his reaction to the differently colored goops, while his highchair hung off the side of the red and white drafting table we used as a dining table. When he started on solid foods, we gave him an avocado for the first time, which he wouldn't eat, but rather squished between his fingers with a look of utter betrayal on his face. I learned recently that this is because babies don't have grip control when they're that young, so they're either holding something with all their strength or not at all. Jason was a pickier eater than I was, which I found to be extremely embarrassing. There was so much good food to eat, I couldn't believe it when he turned his nose up at seafood, at mushrooms, at spicy things (he's over all this now, thank goodness).

It wasn't the intended effect, but all this variety, effort, and education when it came to eating made convenience food an irresistible curiosity for me. I was, and remain, obsessed with TV dinners. A Salisbury Steak Hungry Man signals that I require deep, deep comfort to this day — I love the weird little grill marks, the mirthless mashed potatoes, and the cranberry apple crisp that bubbles over into the green beans every time. I treat Cup O'Noodles like a rare and forbidden delicacy. A frozen chicken pot pie sometimes feels like a gift. I used to beg my mother to buy Hamburger Helper when we were at the grocery store (she never did), because I was obsessed with the commercials on television, and the little cartoon glove mascot.

I finally got to eat Hamburger Helper, down the street at a friend's house. My friend had a Super Nintendo in her bedroom, something that was expressly forbidden in my house, so I assumed that they were probably rich.

This friend had a little sister, and the two of them were often left home alone while both of their parents worked. They had a pet rabbit and a few guinea pigs, and a swing set in the backyard. They taught me to make a sandwich of one piece of white bread, spread thickly with Country Crock margarine and coated with white sugar, and how to clean up so that no one noticed they'd done it, avoiding their father's belt once he got home. Their mom smoked in the house and yelled at them a lot in front of me, and I had no idea how out of place I really was at their dinner table, staring with wonder, down at Hamburger Helper, finally, after all that. It was awful, and I felt terrible for hating it. I felt embarrassed about all the artichokes I'd eaten, and how I'd hungered for the foods I thought were normal, and how I'd had access to something that these girls definitely did not.

I was too young to know that their adults were hurting them in ways that they'd have to carry through the rest of their lives, and too young to begin to understand the privilege that I had. It was one of the few times in my life that food made me feel farther apart from someone, and I was very grateful to go home to our freezer full of Master Sauce.

Cornish Hens in Master Sauce

8 cups of water

1 cup double black soy sauce

2 cup soy sauce

2 cup sherry (Sue calls for sherry, but I always use mirin in mine)

3 tablespoons sugar

1 whole dried chili pepper

1 fresh tangerine peel

5 thick slices of fresh ginger, unpeeled

2 teaspoons whole cloves

2 cinnamon sticks

2 whole star anise

2 large, fresh Cornish hens

Combine all ingredients, except the Cornish hens, and bring to a boil. Lower to simmer. Add the Cornish hens and simmer for an hour or two. Remove the pot from the heat. Let hens sit in the pot, steeping in the sauce, until everything cools down enough to handle.

Strain and freeze master sauce. To use it again, defrost, keeping the fat that rises to the top, replenishing the cinnamon, tangerine peel, and spices.

Can simmer other meats in it too. — Sue Orchant's original recipe note.

Makes 2 quarts of sauce

Rio Rancho: Brownies

To be totally honest, I didn't really get the Girl Scouts. I didn't understand why we were trying to earn badges. I didn't understand why we sold all the cookies but didn't get any money for them, or even any cookies. I hated – and I really can't stress this enough, *hated* – the uniform. The only things I really remember from the experience are the cookies, this craft project we did once where we sewed a stack of newspapers into an oil cloth pouch to make a cushion to sit on (*WTAF?!*), and that godforsaken song.

Make new friends
But keep the old
One is silver
The other is gold
A circle is round
It has no end
That's how long
I will be your friend.

Sweet reader, I ask you: *Why the fuck did we need to learn this song?* What does it even mean? Why is it the national anthem of the Girl Scouts? Do Boy Scouts have to learn songs like this? Or were they getting to build campfires, put tents together, pee in the woods, bake potatoes in hot coals, row boats?

I liked some of the girls in my troupe, and I liked being able to go to their houses for meetings, mostly to see what snacks their parents would make. I liked going to Jessica's house, because she was allowed to have gerbils in her room, and her kitchen had a swinging saloon door that I thought was incredibly fancy.

It was beyond that swinging saloon door, over a plate of orange slices, that I said one of the first really mean things in my life.

This wasn't intentional; I had no beef with Jessica. I liked playing with the rodents she kept as pets, and she had a huge Barbie collection, and anytime my parents came to pick me up from a play date at her house, she and I would hide in her closet, hoping they'd give up and just leave me there. That tradition was about to end abruptly here, in the kitchen, biting into cold citrus.

The meeting was over, parents were on their way to pick up their kids, little groups of seven-year-old girls were clustered around the kitchen and living room. I was standing with Jessica and Tracy, a girl who lived down the street from me who had long, blonde hair, who I thought was beautiful, but sort of mean. It was, perhaps, Tracy's meanness that inspired the thing that happened next.

"So, you're Jewish, right?" Jessica asked me.

"Yeah," I said.

"So, you don't celebrate Christmas, right?" she continued.

"Nope, we have Hanukkah instead."

"So, does that mean you don't believe in Jesus?"

Look, I want to interject here for a second to say that I had already answered these questions about 30 times a year, from the time I left pre-school at Temple Albert in Albuquerque and started kindergarten at Martin Luther King Jr. Elementary in Rio Rancho. Most of the kids I went to school with were Catholic or Baptist, and lots of them had never met another Jew. By this time, in second grade, I'd basically had the answers to these questions tattooed inside my eyelids. I'm telling you this because you're going to, perhaps, find it very hard to believe that what I said next is actually what I said.

"Well," my seven-year-old mouth began, "Jews believe that Jesus existed as a historical person. It's not that we don't believe he was real. We just don't believe that he was the son of God, or that he is the Messiah."

I was aware that I was talking like an adult. I was aware that I was not blonde, that I was not like them, that I was different. I started wearing that as a badge of honor pretty early in my life. When I would tell my parents that someone had called me weird, they would always say the same thing: "Normal is boring. Who wants to be normal?"

Jessica and Tracy made eye contact with each other, then looked back at me. I was peeling the last bit of flesh off of the orange slice in my hands.

"Yeah, well, my mom says that means you're going to hell," Jessica concluded.

I think I knew somewhere in my developing brain that this was Jessica's mom's problem, not hers or mine. And I knew that religion was a sensitive issue for some people, because I'd been learning about the Holocaust since I could fucking form words, but no one had ever used mine against me in this way before, and I felt totally betrayed.

I finished chewing, looked her dead in the eyes and said, "Santa Claus is just your parents buying you presents. Why don't you ask your mom about that?"

I threw away my orange peel and went to find my parents.

It didn't occur to me until very recently what a heavy burden it is for Jewish children to know that Santa isn't real. It was a secret I don't remember being told that I needed to keep, although I'm sure I probably was. This being New Mexico, most of my parents' friends and their kids were gentiles — we mostly spent time around other Jews when we were with our family or at temple. A family friend remarked upon it recently; my brother and I spent Christmas Eve with their family all the time, we helped them decorate their Christmas trees, we opened presents together, knowing all the while that the jolly fellow who brought their presents down the chimney was 100% their mom and dad, and we never — for a second — considered spilling the beans. I certainly hadn't ever considered using this information as ammunition before. Something about Jessica's tone of voice made me weaponize Santa that day.

I got one of my first very serious talking-tos from my dad after what I said to Jessica in her kitchen. I was, understandably, upset that her antisemitism wasn't being taken more seriously than my cruel, if justifiable, response. I didn't have those words at that age, but I did understand that you weren't supposed to treat someone else's religious beliefs like that, and that you weren't really supposed to talk to people like that.

"All I did was tell her Santa isn't real. She said I was going to hell."

"Right," Marc Orchant said to me, "But you already know that hell isn't real."

He didn't really say explicitly that sometimes it is more important to be compassionate rather than right. He also didn't say that it wasn't okay to be mean just because I was smart. And he *certainly* wouldn't have said that being different would make people say weird shit to me for the rest of my life, and I couldn't lose my fucking mind every single time it happened. But looking back on it, I think that's what he meant. I really wish I could ask him if he remembers this.

Provincetown: Someone Else's Oyster Stew

DECEMBER 29, 2020

I know you feel it too. We've come to the end of another year. A designation as arbitrary as anything I can think of.

In truth, "a year" is a human construct meant to help us organize our thoughts and feelings. We need structure more than almost any other species on this rock (ants maybe have us beat), and we decided, somewhere along the way, that it made sense to segment our time into easily digestible chunks. Chunks we can call "great," or "unremarkable," or "absolutely cursed." And as always happens, at the end of said easily digestible chunk of time, we are encouraged to look back at our accomplishments, our failures, at the things we loved most, or the things we think we'll always remember. Throw that idea out the fucking window.

Like Joan Didion leaving New York, saying "Goodbye to All That," with respect to my eternal literary hero: fuck all that. *Truly, fuck all that.*

If we know anything at all, after the years we've managed to live through so far, it's that, in reality — that terrible space we have had to violently remind ourselves back into for months — at midnight on January 1st, when our internal calendars and digital calendars and analog calendars slip unremarkably from 2020 to 2021, whether we toast gleefully or somberly, whether we rage-dance in our living rooms or sleep through it, everything that has been totally and unrelentingly fucked will remain so. Totally and unrelentingly fucked. To quote one of my father's favorite acronyms, "FUBAR." Fucked up beyond all recognition.

There. Doesn't that feel better? To just admit it and get it over with?

Sure, have hope. Oh my god, by all means, have hope. Unless you can't, which would be understandable. Or, be filled with unholy rage. Let that rage radicalize you. Let it shove you out the gate. Let it make you protect people more vulnerable than you, by any means necessary. By all means. But you — you there, wrapped in the blanket on the couch — do you feel hopeless? Do you feel lost? Do you feel unmoored? Are you having trouble imagining things getting any better ever again? Do you feel rage, and hope, and sorrow, and regret, and gratitude, and still feel like none of them are enough to make you take off the blanket?

Same here, friend. I don't really know what to do about it, but I do know where to start.

Like M.F.K. Fisher, who is tied for first place with Didion for "things I wish I'd thought of," I really and truly believe there is only one viable place to begin: "First we eat, then we do everything else."

I know that sounds dumb as hell when there is so much collateral damage from the world. But I trust her. She lived through a global pandemic, the Great Depression, world wars, loss of loved ones, and came out on the other side with that purely distilled philosophy.

"First we eat, then we do everything else."

Today, I was digging around for one of her many oyster stew recipes in Consider the Oyster. I have, of course, either lent or given away every copy of it I've ever owned, anxious for everyone to get to feel the feeling of reading it for the first time. I was looking for it, because I think that soup is where we start. Instead, I found a copy of

With Bold Knife & Fork. In it, a chapter about soup — as a fortifier, as palliative care, "as the main course of a long, gabby supper, with plenty of pumpernickel and ripe cheeses, or after a lengthy session of music and more talk, when people begin to feel a predawn intimation that they are not immortal."

She goes on, immediately, to describe the best soup she ever ate, in April or May of 1921.

> *I had been in bed for perhaps five days with some kind of flu, and except for an occasional remote word of sympathy from my parents, who had to remain antiseptic because of all the younger siblings and who therefore could get no closer to me than it takes to use a thermometer, I was alone; even my sister had been moved relentlessly to the spare room.*

Let us, my dear ones, be extremely honest about this one thing: If I had read this sentence in 2019, it wouldn't have meant much to me. It would have registered as old-fashioned, and as a nod to fewer vaccines, less-understood epidemiological research, and as a sign of how many goddamned siblings she had. Today I read that sentence and it fucking leveled me. By 1921, the specter of the 1918 H1N1 pandemic would still have been looming. The shock of the experience would still feel palpable. After the third wave of that global pandemic in late 1919, her parents were afraid, like everyone would have been, that it could start all over again at any moment.

But then, on day five, once she's drunk as much watered-down juice as her fever needed to break, she smells beef broth wafting up from downstairs. Her dad comes home from work and gives her a "bone cracking hug." She despairs, afraid that might be all she gets for the day, once she hears everyone gather for lunch in the dining room.

"He had not reminded them that I lay alone — weak, starved, almost sobbing, alive."

> *And then my mother came. She put down a little tray with a big bowl on it and gave me the second hug of the week and my first kiss and went away. There, alone with me, waiting for me, was the biggest bowl — a kitchen bowl — of the most beautiful soup I had ever seen or smelled, of a clear color like strong tea, with other glowing colors not too far below the surface, and a pearly vapor rising straight up.*

She eats the first few bites with a spoon, then, knowing it's what her mother intended, she picks up the giant bowl with her little hands, and tips it back, and gulps it down like a "half-drowned cow or sailor will suck at the air." She knows that, fortified by two hugs, one kiss, and a kitchen-bowl of soup, she is on her way back to normalcy. That there will be more of each of them soon.

She goes on to get on airplanes and steamships, to eat lavish meals in the peaks of the Alps, to cook arguably more satisfying ones on a single hot plate in a cramped apartment in France with one of the loves of her life, to have children, to live in California, to publish books, to be all the way alive. And so will we. But first, we have to eat something.

This is not M.F.K. Fisher's oyster stew recipe. In fact, I suspect that *she* would tell you that her recipe wasn't hers. This recipe was Mischa's when he fed it to Kiah on his porch one day. Then, it became Kiah's when she made it for us on Christmas Eve in Ben and Tess's kitchen. Next, it will be yours, when you feed it to someone who is hungry, and cold, and maybe a little unmoored.

There are as many versions of this stew as there are oyster shells. I've always used cream for the stew until now, and I balked at the coconut milk. I was suspicious right up until I ate it — the first few bites with a spoon, to extract each oyster in the steaming mug, and then, with two hands, like a half-drowned cow.

Kiah's Oyster Stew

1 pint freshly shucked oysters and their liquor
4 shallots, minced
1 head garlic, minced
6-ish sprigs thyme
2 14oz. cans coconut milk
Salt and pepper
Olive oil

Sauté shallots in a bit of olive oil over medium heat, until they soften up and turn translucent. Add garlic and thyme, and cook until the garlic is fragrant, but not brown.

Add coconut milk, and heat until it just starts to boil. Whack the heat way down to a gentle simmer and add the oysters and their liquor. Cook only until the oysters are warmed through, and just starting to curl around the edges.

Taste before you season (oyster liquor is just very special salt water, you may not need any extra) with salt and pepper. Spoon a few oysters into each mug or bowl, then pour the hot soup over them. Serve absolutely immediately.

Serves 4 as a starter

Albuquerque: Lori's Café

Somewhere between late elementary school and early middle school, my dad worked for a graphic design and printing company in Albuquerque. It was a family business, and I spent many afternoons after school, before Hebrew school, or on sick days, curled up on two chairs pushed together like a tiny makeshift couch. On most of these days, I'd do homework listening to my portable CD player, while my dad went gliding around the office "putting out fires," as he liked to say. They had just started getting into large-format printing, and there was one great big, ink- and-toner-smelling white room, with huge ceilings and the constant whir of printers the size of entire rooms in our house.

I just looked up the business, which is no longer in existence, and was reminded of his email signature during those times — "Sanity is the playground for the unimaginative." You really couldn't have made that guy up.

I was frequently bored there, hoping for the clock to run down so we could go home, and I could do basically the exact same thing, but in my own bedroom. But lunchtime was a different story.

In this mostly beige, unremarkable office park (truly the stuff that my current nightmares are made of), there was a cafe that functioned as a company cafeteria for all the businesses there. It was called Lori's Cafe and I recall there being a German woman there, who either owned it, or did enough that she should have. I'm relatively sure this was Lori, but my brain is playing tricks on me with this memory (my mom had to remind me that it was not, in fact, called Lupe's Cafe).

I recall, for some reason, there being a huge photographic mural of a meadow with a waterfall that took up one entire wall, and there being a TV mounted in one corner near the ceiling. It was a very typical New Mexican cafe, by which I mean that you could get a bowl of green chile stew, or a plate of enchiladas, but you could also just have, like, a ham and cheese on a Kaiser roll or a chef salad.

For me, and I feel like this won't surprise anyone, it was always grilled cheese. This particular grilled cheese was on white bread, with gooey, yellow American cheese. It was always cut diagonally into triangles (again, the uncontested champion), set on a Styrofoam plate next to a plastic condiment cup of neon green pickle chips, and summarily wrapped, still steaming hot, in plastic wrap, presumably, to keep it hot on the two-minute walk back to my dad's office.

It sounds objectively revolting, but somehow, that warming plastic wrap smell got tangled up in my scent memory of this ultimate comfort food. Although it probably poisoned my brain a little, anytime I get a really good diner grilled cheese — which is to say, absolutely any time it's available to me, the kind you can only make on a flat top seasoned by years of burgers and eggs — I think of Lori's Cafe, and my dad, and that strange little office where everyone knew my name.

Maybe because I was kind of a tiny adult in a way that made regular adults laugh, or maybe because I so enthusiastically loved this grilled cheese, there were a few times when Lori would bring me back into that kitchen, in front of that enormous flat top, and show me how to do things. She let me ladle pancake batter onto the griddle and try my hardest to flip them without messing them up. She showed me the secret to the even browning on that grilled cheese, spreading what I am quite sure was room temperature margarine onto the whole surface of the bread before it touched the griddle, and how to *smoosh* it a little to get it to melt faster, but not so much that it got flat. I was always nervous during these encounters, eager to get back to the comparative sanctuary of my dad's office and, like, the Green Day CD I was listening to on repeat (*OH, GODDD!*), but I did think that it was pretty cool to have a job where you just cooked all day long.

Lori never made me get into the dish pit, or clean a grease trap, or even try to sweep ice off a linoleum floor, but she showed me the parts that made me think about cooking on a giant griddle forever. I still crave neon pickle chips all the time.

Albuquerque: Ski Cheese

I don't have the kind of grandmother who calls you "baby." She doesn't scoop you into her bosom when you're scared. She doesn't smell like cookies. Glenda smells like Obsession by Calvin Klein.

It doesn't really matter what situation she is in – my grandmother is in charge. She is decisive, and she does not have time for nonsense. I was born on the first night of Passover, so she set up a Seder table in the hallway at Presbyterian Hospital in Albuquerque, New Mexico to welcome me into the world. Once, I put sugar in her coffee as a joke, and she spat it back into the cup while she made eye contact with me, sort of like a lioness lining up for a kill. On another occasion, I brought a cheeseburger to Hebrew school (a major Kashrut no-no), where she was the Director of Education, and she threw me out of the building with a single, wordless glance.

Eating with my grandmother was sometimes a game of chess. She always wanted me to eat more than I could, to try things I was afraid of, and to act like a tiny adult (there's a theme here, it seems). We were sitting next to each other at a French restaurant when I was probably six or seven and Glenda held out her miniature fork, after deftly prying loose what I had no idea at that moment was a snail.

"Try this," she said, and I didn't even realize I could say no. I knew then that I was in over my head, that I'd have to do it. It also helped that I was already very interested in things cooked in butter and garlic and was smart enough to recognize their smell.

After I chewed and swallowed my first ever bite of escargot, Glenda asked, "Did you like that?"

I nodded my head, yes.

"Do you want to know what it was?"

I nodded my head, yes.

"It's called escargot in French. Do you know what that is?"

I shook my head, no.

"They're snails. Would you like another one?"

I shook my head, no. What had this woman gotten me into?

"Are you sure?" she asked, as I continued to smell garlic and butter.

"I'll try one more," I said.

"Good girl," she said.

When I was young, Glenda had a hairdresser named Buddy who came to her house nearly every morning to twist her salt and pepper hair into a sleek chignon while she sat in a dining chair next to the grand piano in her living room. This happened with such frequency and regularity, that I didn't realize her hair came down past her shoulders until I was an adult, even though I used to watch Buddy work his magic from my seat at the kitchen table multiple times a week.

My grandmother cracks T-bones between her teeth at the table to suck out the marrow. Her smile, when she really laughs, seems to take up the entire width of her head. My grandmother shows her affection by biting the end of your nose until you think she's going to draw blood. Sometimes she hugs you so hard you think you'll pass out. She makes you earn your seat at the table by quizzing you on current events. And she makes you sit down and talk with each other by making a cheese plate.

Norm and Glenda's living room was the communal meeting place of my youth. It's where we sat before and after dinner, before and after breaking the fast, before and after Shabbat services. There was a wood and mother-of-pearl inlaid box that contained a checkers and chess set, on a long, low, stone-topped coffee table, which was always punctuated on one end by one of those enormous, layered tins of assorted cookies in their own little paper cups, and on the other by a cheese board of some seriousness. Half of us would sit on the big, pillowy, pastel couch — it was a huge L-shaped sectional, which for some reason I thought was the pinnacle of luxury — and half of us on the floor, the best spots for access to this ubiquitous combination of cheese, crackers, and pickled things.

There was a passthrough over the couch into the kitchen, which she used to keep one eye on us while she cooked, and one eye on the tiny TV on the counter that always somehow had a baseball game on it. For some time, there was also a birdcage on the counter, where a parakeet named Harpo lived, always squawking out "BOKER TOV," (Hebrew for "good morning") or "NORMAN!" — the two things Glenda shouts the most.

I used to think that my family was a special kind of strange, until I spent enough time in other people's families to realize that everyone has the difficult ones, the easy ones, the allies, the outliers, the one who helps do the dishes, the one who chews with their mouth open, the one who has never gotten over the fight at the breakfast table when they were 11, the one who always has to be right. My dad's three siblings and their spouses were often around, even though most of them lived across the country, and it was at this gathering place around the cheese board that I remember watching them be most happy to interact.

There was always something hard and sharp (I mean cheese, but also obviously people) with a small, forked knife, something pungent and soft with a broad, squat knife, and nearly every time, a caramel brown cube of Gjetost — always referred to in her house as Ski Cheese — with a small cheese plane, meant to lay flat on the cheese, and drag down its surface, making a perfectly thin slice. Gjetost is a Norwegian goat and cow's milk cheese that's made by cooking down whey until it caramelizes, and then compressing it into a dense, fudge-like cube. I loved peeling off the red Ski Queen label with the little illustration of a cheese plane, slicing off a curl. It felt like a present from somewhere far away. The flavor is intense, almost more dessert than it is cheese, and I never made it more than one slice in before turning my attention back to the Gouda or the Brie. Thinking back on it, I have no idea who even liked this cheese, or why it was always there, but it's the one I remember most because I was so bewildered by it. Glenda and Norm's eldest, Marc was usually the ringleader for nostalgic story time around the cheese board.

It really cannot be overstated how funny my dad was. Part of it was because he was so smart, and so proud of his fluency in sarcasm, but a lot of it had to do with his perfect, unquestionably rehearsed comedic timing. Once, he made my best friend Ashleigh laugh so hard at the dinner table that Dr. Pepper rocketed out of her nostrils. When we were with family, he'd tell the story about the time on summer vacation in Spain, when everyone thought he and my uncle Ed had been kidnapped because they stayed at the beach for so long, eating grilled sardines and octopus. He'd start the story about Chaucer, the Cairn terrier of their youth, getting into my uncle Craig's medication and losing his mind, or maybe getting squashed by Alison when she fell down the stairs — before all three of the others, Ed, Craig, and Alison would jump in to correct his memory and defend their own innocence with respect to Chaucer's untimely demise.

There were always dogs around: Simcha, their beloved Westie who was gentle and affectionate, was my favorite. There were also Keeshonds — Keesha who was sweet and timid, and Smoky before her, who was so smart they had to put child locks on all the cabinets in the kitchen to keep him out, and so rambunctious that I once chipped a tooth on their brick entryway trying to outrun his chase. Later, there was a Scottie, MacDougal, that my grandfather loved like he loves chocolate and golf, which is to say, more than almost anything else on Earth. Although the food was always down near their grasp, I rarely remember them stealing any. There was also an awful Persian cat called Toolie (short for *chatul,* which means "cat" in Hebrew) who spent nearly her entire flat-faced life cowering under my grandparents' bed, save the times that Glenda would drag her out into the dining room and force us all to say how pretty she was.

"Isn't she just the most beautiful thing you've *ever seen?*" she insisted, laughing, at once sarcastic and deadly serious, while Toolie scratched at her, trying desperately to escape.

Now, they have a rescue named Rocky, who is sweet and goofy and not big enough to pull on them too much when they take him for walks around their apartment complex in northern New Jersey, where they live so that they can be close to my aunts and uncles, and which my grandfather has just recently stopped referring to as "a prison." They're usually too tired to entertain, aside from playing bridge once a week with some friends, and most of their meals are prepared by caretakers or eaten out at restaurants.

But at Norm and Glenda's house in Albuquerque, meals were always multi-coursed and elaborate, even if it was just me and my parents in attendance. There was always a first course of either a half a grapefruit, with a knife run around all the segments, or a slice of cantaloupe, bite-sized chunks already pre-cut into them and laid back into the crescent of the rind, so that they were easier to eat politely at the table. For Passover Seders, which were always at Norm and Glenda's, there was a choice between gefilte fish or chopped liver, both served on a leaf of lettuce with horseradish. There was often a soup course – matzoh ball for holidays, of course, and in the summer, there was gazpacho served with little dishes of chopped up cucumbers, peppers and onions, so you could add as much as you liked. But my favorite soup at Glenda's was split pea, heavy with marrow bones and barley. It seemed like everyone always wanted their food to be boneless in those days – be it chicken breasts or fish filets – but here Glenda was actively adding them back in, because they made soup taste better and gave her an opportunity to take a crack at them at the table.

"Oh, I just used the Manischewitz soup mix, and tossed some marrow bones in there," she revealed to me sometime later. "There were always so many other things to do."

There were latkes to be fried, always in the twin electric skillets that I only ever saw used for this very purpose. There was brisket to braise. Kugel to check on in the oven. Sweet potatoes to be pureed with crème fraîche. I'm often struck by the incredible privilege of being born into a family that loves food and has the means to make so much of it. I can only remember Glenda making me eat two objectively disgusting things: 1) a peanut butter and jelly sandwich that she sent me to school with, wrapped in tin foil and inexplicably made on two slices of kalamata olive bread, and 2) Kashi puffed rice cereal in 2% milk, which might as well just be cardboard pellets soaked in dishwater.

I don't remember helping a lot in Glenda's kitchen when I was young, because the counters seemed very tall, but I do remember being tasked with carrying plates to the table, setting the places, rolling the cloth napkins into the napkin rings, often themed little ceramic pieces in the shape of vegetables, or rabbits. There was a bar cart in the dining room with big brass wheels that I always thought looked like Cinderella's coach. There were big sliding glass doors that opened onto a brick patio, which hung off the back of that house in the foothills of the Sandias, from which you could see the entire city of Albuquerque, lights twinkling, a lot more glamorous from that altitude.

I've been dreaming of this house a lot lately. Mostly that I'm there for a party, but that I leave the crowded dining room and wander down the hall, peeking into the den to see my grandpa sitting in the big blue leather recliner, watching golf and ignoring the cocktail chatter. Or slipping into my aunt's old bedroom, to sit on her daybed and look at the dolls my grandmother collected any time they traveled the world. Or, wandering into Norm and Glenda's bedroom, where the heavy, embroidered floral curtains blocked out most of the light, and you could walk into the closet, close the wooden shuttered door, and smell nothing but mothballs and Obsession by Calvin Klein while you let the clothes hold up the weight of your whole, still very small body.

When I was in high school, Glenda hired me and my best friend to cater a ladies' luncheon. I have no idea why she did this, or what even gave her the idea, but I do remember Ashleigh and I had a meeting with her to discuss a menu theme: "Springy, nothing too heavy, make a lot of salads — that will make them happy." We planned the menu, figured out how much food we'd need to buy to feed 10 or 15 people, and presented her with a budget. It was the first menu planning and food-costing I'd ever done, and I have no memory of how it turned out, which means that it was probably just fine. I know there was a couscous salad, a big bowl of leafy greens in vinaigrette, and a Mediterranean chicken salad from the *Silver Palate Cookbook* with capers and Kalamata olives that we poached and shredded the breasts for ourselves.

I remember thinking that it was a pretty decent way to make enough money to go to the mall with, and it's probably responsible for more of the professional choices I've made in my life than I realize.

Albuquerque: Becky

My first job in a restaurant was in a sushi bar in Albuquerque, owned by a Korean sushi chef named Tom.

I'd never waited tables before, but my family and I used to eat there a few times a month. I'd memorized the whole menu, and I was eager to have serving experience for when I went off to college. Tom always smiled when we came in for lunch or dinner, he remembered everyone's names, and I was disproportionately excited to exercise my small employee discount.

The uniform was all black, so I bought black dress pants, black Converse low-tops, and a few plain, black shirts. They gave me a black half-apron to wear on my first day, and told me to shadow with the hostess, Nicole, the only other white girl who worked there. After a few days, when I'd understood the reservation book and answered the phone whenever it rang, I got to put the complimentary miso soups together in the kitchen: a few cubes of tofu in each bowl, a few sliced scallions, and then a few ladles of miso from the huge crockpot between the sushi bar and the hot line, making sure to scoop a few pieces of seaweed into each bowl with the hot soup. They all went onto a small, cork-topped tray, and you tried your best not to make a mess on your way to the table.

This kind of restaurant work seemed easier and lower stakes to me than working at The Olive Garden or something, where the room was huge, the plates were big and hot, and the trays weighed as much as I did. I confirmed this suspicion for myself later in life, when I hosted at a Buca di Beppo, giving parties of 10 a tour through the kitchen on every visit, and burning myself absolutely every time I ran food, the plates always blistering hot and piled with 10 pounds of Pasta alla Norma.

Here, at the sushi bar, the only hot things we ever had to carry were soup and green tea, the customers marked their orders on a little checklist, so you never had to remember anything except drink orders, and the sushi chefs barked the hot line orders to Ta, the Vietnamese grandpa who was often smoking a cigarette next to the fryer in the kitchen. When your shrimp tempura or firecracker squid salad were ready, they'd appear behind the sushi bar, and one of the quiet, kind sushi chefs would silently make eye contact with you to come and get it. My favorite one, the pony-tailed Japanese veteran Tanaka, was objectively hilarious, constantly cracking inside jokes with customers seated at the bar, absolutely *screaming* "IRASSHAIMASE!" when anyone walked into the restaurant, who was always ready to cheer us up when a customer, or more often the owner, was acting like a complete asshole.

The restaurant had a teppan-yaki side also — the long, griddle tables where the chefs put on a pyrotechnics show, a comedy show, and also seared steaks to temperature while they remembered the orders of everyone around the table. I was never allowed to work on that side of the restaurant. That side of the restaurant belonged to the Korean head waitress, Jian, and her two proteges, So-Young and Sookyung, who went by Rachel because she justifiably hated the way English-speakers pronounced her name: "It's like your mouths don't understand."

Beyond the teppan tables, there were huge swinging doors into what I now understand to be an absolutely gigantic prep kitchen.

Stainless steel industrial refrigerators lined the walls, with six sparkling steel prep tables between them. I worked the dinner shift, so I never really got to be in the big kitchen while prep was happening, but a few times I got to slice the scallions for the miso soup, while all four Filipino teppan chefs made fun of my knife skills.

"How did you guys learn to slice them so thin?" I asked, earnestly.

"Oh, school," one of them said.

"Really?"

And they all laughed hysterically.

"No, you just have to practice."

They showed me how to hold the knife between my right thumb and index finger, and how to keep my left fingertips curled under my knuckles and away from the knife's edge. They were all in their twenties, and a few of them were cute, and I'm grateful that I was not yet 18 and able to make any bad decisions with them. The four of them always seemed to be together, and although they were definitely flirting with me, they also seemed protective of me — shouting at Ta to "fuck off" when he stared at my ass, walking me to my car at night, telling me all the ingredients to the salad dressing when I couldn't remember.

Family meals at this restaurant ended up being the major highlight of my time working there. Everyone who could be trusted to make enough food quickly took turns at the helm, and it felt like every one of them made you the thing they liked the best. The teppan chefs usually made noodles, fried on the teppan tables in huge batches, with thinly sliced, extra marinated bits of pork and green onions. When it was Tom or Tanaka's turn, we'd get to eat sushi — they'd try out new sushi roll ideas on us, broil us a hamachi kama to split greedy bites of, and ask which sashimi we hadn't yet tried. When it was Ta's turn, he always made a stir-fry, usually of celery, cucumbers, chicken and chili paste (I've never encountered this exact dish anywhere ever again, despite always being on the lookout).

Jian generally scowled in my direction any time I made a sound, and I always wanted her to like me better than she did. She had a huge laugh, wore hot pink lipstick, permed her hair, and treated customers like friends, even if she'd never seen them before. But her patience with me was paper-thin from the start. She rolled her eyes when I asked her questions, she openly mocked me in Korean when I couldn't do the math on the tips in my head, and she called me "Becky" — a nickname I despise — any chance she got. The first time I got to eat Jian's staff meal, she made kalbi, rice, and stir-fried vegetables. I hadn't had much experience with Korean food before, but the ingredients were familiar, and I always made sure to clean my plate at family meals. The short ribs were sweet, and sticky, and didn't put up much of a fight between my teeth and my chopsticks as I tore them off the little bit of bone. Jian scowled at me.

"Where'd you learn to use chopsticks like that, Becky?"

I shrugged, "My parents taught me when I was really little."

Her eyes narrowed, she got up from the table, and went into the prep kitchen wordlessly. I raised my eyebrows in Tom's direction to see if I'd done something wrong. He snorted a little and continued to eat. Jian returned a moment later with a rectangular Tupperware container that she set down in front of me on the table. The teppan chefs all started laughing and whooping. Jian opened the Tupperware to reveal what looked like grape leaves in a thick, oily brine, with hoops of chilies floating around on top. This was a dare.

"What's that?" I asked.

"It's healthy for you," she said. "See if you can handle it."

She rolled one of the leaves up like a cigarette with a pair of chopsticks and held it out to me. I grasped the bundle with my chopsticks and put the whole thing in my mouth. These turned out to be perilla leaf kimchi, and to say that I was unprepared for the entire fireworks store-worth of flavors that were about to explode in my face would be a grave understatement. My eyes widened visibly — how could something be so spicy, sour, astringent, salty, scratchy, and minty at once? They had the effervescence of a really sour pickle, stung my tongue, and cleared my sinuses.

"What is that?" I repeated.

"I said it's healthy for you," Jian said again, confirming that I'd have to figure it out on my own.

"Can I have another one, please?"

I think it's the only time she ever smiled at me without saying something mean.

Things went along smoothly for a while. It was the furthest out of my cultural element I'd ever been but growing up as the only Jewish kid in a New Mexican elementary school had given me some sense of how to act. When the staff was speaking to each other in Korean, I thought about school, and about boys, and about whatever monologue I was trying to memorize for theater class. Occasionally Tom would scream a direction at me in Korean, and then, with a frustrated sigh, translate it to English. I tried to be polite, to do my work, to be friendly but not annoying. One night I broke two glasses in a row while bussing a table and felt Tom's eyes burn into me.

"I'm sorry!" I mouthed across the room.

"If you break another glass, your tips will pay for it," he said, as he passed me while I swept up the mess.

Then Nicole, the hostess, quit. She called just before family meal was about to start to say she wouldn't be coming that night, or ever again. Tom shouted at her on the phone outside for a few minutes, before he came in to announce it to everyone. He pointed to me.

"You, come with me."

I followed him to the hostess stand, wondering what I'd done.

"You're working the hostess stand, until we can get another one."

I was so disappointed. The hostess never got tipped out from the tip pool, but it was about more than that. It meant I didn't get to do any prep work in the kitchen, that Ta couldn't hand me an extra fried shrimp when I passed him on the hot line, that I wouldn't hear Tanaka's jokes at the sushi bar, that I couldn't sip on a little mug of miso soup when I got hungry halfway through my shift. I was being demoted, and I knew it, and I could feel why. But I wanted to keep my job, and I could tell he was upset, so I just agreed.

"Don't ever quit a job like this," he said. "This is always how white girls quit. It really pisses me off. You think you can just walk away, and it doesn't affect everyone else. It's so rude. It's always how it happens. It really pisses me off."

I didn't think I deserved to get lectured about quitting a job that I hadn't, but I also didn't think I was in any position to argue with him. I hadn't worked the hostess stand since I'd started the job months before, so the first night was a little rocky, but there weren't many reservations, and I didn't make any big mistakes.

During the last hour of dinner service, Jian passed the hostess stand and said, "Make another pot of coffee."

It was the one task Nicole always handled, and I realized I'd never been taught how to do it. Jian was already way out of earshot, and I loathed asking her for help with anything, so I just went over to the huge, industrial coffeemaker and stared at it for a minute. It was taller than I was, I had no idea where the coffee was, and I figured I was probably on my way to a steam burn. As an innately clumsy person, I knew better than to approach a machine that dispensed boiling water with anything less than reverence. I looked for So-Young, because she was always nice when I was lost, but she was all the way across the teppan side of the restaurant.

"What's the problem?" Jian asked from behind me.

"I've just never done this before," I said.

"So what?" She asked.

"Well, no one ever taught me how to do it, and I didn't want to mess it up."

She used one arm to push me aside, and the other to pull down the brewing basket and do it herself.

"Remind me to tell Tom to never hire another white girl again," she said.

My face got really hot, and I felt like I was going to cry, like I often do when I'm really angry in a situation I'm not supposed to get angry in. I went back to the hostess stand with my lip quivering, and made silverware roll-ups until we were closed, and the tips were counted. I didn't get any, as I knew I wouldn't, and I left without saying goodnight to anyone.

I was more upset by being singled out for my whiteness than I was about the demotion in pay and position. It felt horrible to be punished for someone else's actions just because we looked the same, and I hadn't thought that anything about my abilities, or work ethic, or behavior had been the same as Nicole's. I was so hurt and frustrated by it in the moment, but I'm exceedingly grateful for it now.

This is, of course, a painfully common experience for anyone who isn't white and cisgender, that the color of my skin and straight-passing privilege usually protect me from. I can still feel the anger and pain it inspired so palpably, and it's something I've carried through every moment of the time I've been responsible for managing other people. I never want to make anyone feel like that or let anyone else make someone feel like that in my presence, and I really hope I never have. It feels like it's probably a lot easier to utterly fail at this if you've never felt it first-hand before.

The next day, because I was 17 and angry, I did the shittiest thing I could possibly imagine and quit exactly the way Nicole had the day before. I called in the afternoon, hours before family meal, to tell Tom what Jian had said to me, how I felt stupid, and out of place, and like no one wanted me there, and that I wouldn't be coming in ever again.

He shouted the same things at me that he had the night before, the same things he'd shouted at Nicole, said that he should have known better, and that I was rude and selfish – which, at the time, was absolutely true. I had just confirmed for him that he was right: We were all the same.

I never saw any of those people again after that night, and it was many years before I ever got to dig my chopsticks into the crevices of a broiled hamachi kama again.

Manhattan: Just Be Cool, Kid

There is a chapter in M.F.K. Fisher's *The Gastronomical Me* in which she describes one of the first restaurant meals she and her first husband had when they moved to Dijon. For the celebration of their first month of marriage, their landlady recommended a restaurant in the town center, Ribodaut's – behind another restaurant, up a set of stairs, which you enter through the kitchen hallway, before ending up in a small, plain dining room. Fisher and her husband could never have found it on their own, and even had to stop to ask the owner of another restaurant for directions.

> *The man laughed again, gave us a silent little push toward the light, and disappeared. We never saw him after, but I remember how pleased he seemed to be, to leave his own café for a minute and direct such obviously bemazed innocents upstairs to Ribodaut's. Probably, it had never occurred to him, a good Burgundian, that anyone in the world did not know exactly how to come from any part of it, straight to the famous door.*
>
> *The first meal we had was a shy stupid one, but even if we had never gone back and never learned gradually how to order food and wine, it would still be among the important ones of my life.*

They're blessed to be taken under the wing of Charles, an experienced and gifted server – something you can't fully appreciate until it's happened to you – who helped guide them through their first *prix fixe,* recommending that they begin the meal with a half-carafe of the house white wine for their first courses, and moving on to a full carafe of the house red.

"That was the only time Charles ever did that, but I have always blessed him for it," she notes. "One of the great wines, which I have watched other people order there through snobbism or timidity when they knew as little as we did, would have been utterly wasted on us. Charles started us out right, and through the months watched us with his certain deft guidance learn to know what wine we wanted, and why."

This is how I think about my Uncle Mitch. He came into my life when my dear Aunt Alison gleefully eloped with him in the late 1990s. My dad's baby sister, she and I are exactly 20 years apart, and I have always held a special spot in my heart for her, somewhere between family and friends. As a child, I used to stay with her and her first husband Paul in their house near the university. They had two cats (who I was terrified of), an Italian Greyhound named Benny (who I loved like a brother), a few garter snakes, and — as I remember it — a hammock in the living room for a time. Looking back on their odd menagerie in that adobe casita on Bryn Mawr Street, I wondered aloud what my former uncle was doing while my aunt studiously toiled away in law school.

"We had snakes in the living room, Rebecca. Paul was a drug dealer," she clarified recently, as if it were the most obvious thing in the world. It probably should have been.

When they got divorced, I thought like most children and others cursed with naivete that it was the worst thing that could ever happen. I knew she was devastated. I knew she and my dad had a lot of long conversations about it. And I knew she was moving to New York, which in turn devastated me. But since it was where most of my family still lived, and since we visited at least once a year, I decided, with the false importance children are notorious for, that I would live with this decision if it was better for her.

Then she moved to New York and started her real life. She became a more independent and tenacious version of herself than I think she expected to, a fact which absolutely did not surprise my dad. And then she met Mitch, and has eaten and drunk better for it for the rest of her life, as a result. So have we, as a matter of fact, and although he is sometimes incredibly annoying, I think we're all very lucky. Sometimes divorce is something to celebrate.

When I was 16, Ali and Mitch took me to Lupa Osteria Romana in Greenwich Village. I was already well-obsessed with food, but surely didn't know what I was talking about or how to order in a restaurant very well. I remember that we started with a little dish of olives — gigantic green Cerignolas, teeny tiny Arbequiñas cured in salt, pink Gaetas I'd never seen before — all bathed in oil and citrus and rosemary. There was also a small dish of elder Parmigiano Reggiano, simply cut into chunks and served that way, with bread, and a ramekin of the best and fruitiest olive oil I had ever tasted.

I looked over the menu, not with panic like it sometimes befalls us in new situations, but with an electric awareness that I was going to eat something really special. It was dark and candle-lit in the room, which made everyone look beautiful, and lent a tiny cushion of privacy to how fast my eyes were darting over the menu. Mitch asked what I was having, and I responded probably more casually than I felt. I don't remember what I ordered all those years ago, but I do remember that after we'd gone around the table and given our orders to our server (*who didn't even write anything down...oh my god how is he going to remember all of that?* — but of course, he did), Mitch ordered the wine.

I love when Mitch orders the wine, even now, when I am the one who orders the wine anytime he is not there. Mitch has very good taste in wine, and even more than that, an entertainingly out-sized bravado about asking for it — he's never met a server he hasn't antagonized, but somehow it usually endears them (and us) to him even more.

"How many glasses should I bring?" asked our server.

"Three, please," said Mitch, closing the wine list and handing it over, popping an olive in his mouth and grinning.

There is no way this is going to work, I thought, with one eyebrow cocked. I grew up in Albuquerque, where you get carded if you are so much as next to someone buying alcohol, and I couldn't possibly imagine getting served a glass of wine in a restaurant this nice.

It turns out that in New York City in 2000, that was not the case.

As the server came around with glasses, three of them, set in front of each of us with a careful flourish, I felt like fireworks were about to shoot out of my ears. My aunt smiled a little smile at me that read *just be cool, kid,* and I did my best. Our server poured Mitch a taste, while he talked through the vintage and the region — unintelligible to me at the time, but I was rapt nevertheless — Mitch took a sniff, a swig, smiled and said, "FANTASTIC," in his way which either means it's fucking fantastic, or you've really biffed it and served him some trash. (My favorite variation on this technique is "Fascinating!" which means either that it's fascinating or more likely that it's the most tedious bullshit he's ever heard, with only context and tone to guide you — like some kind of middle-aged-Jewish-man-click-language.) In this case he was pleased, and our server made his way around to my aunt's glass, then mine, then Mitch's, before he set the bottle down in the middle of his table and went on his way.

"Cheers, cutie," they said, and raised their glasses. It's important to note that until that exact moment, the wine I'd consumed to that point in my life consisted of as many shots of Kosher wine after Shabbat services as it took to get a buzz on, a swallow of whatever was leftover in the fridge after my parents had a party, and probably a few sips of champagne on New Year's Eve.

I don't know which varietal was in my glass that night, it might have been a Montalcino or a Sangiovese, but it was certainly the best wine I'd ever tasted in my young life. It hit my tongue with goddamn *pizzazz* — there wasn't a hint of sourness, it had the texture of velvet, and it made effervescence sparkle across my taste buds. I didn't know shit about top notes, or noses, or legs; it didn't matter, because I had just tasted something supremely delicious. It got better when the food came, the food I don't even remember because I was so high on being treated like an adult for one of the first times. And also, probably a little buzzed.

The interior walls of the restaurant were a lush, warm orange — the same color as their business card, which I dutifully rubber-cemented into my journal after this meal and did probably some of the first food writing I'd ever done, absolutely freaked out by how delicious food could be, how luxurious dining could be, and how good wine could taste.

It's impossible to discuss this blessed memory without noting that this restaurant was formerly owned by a celebrity chef who had a most public and hideous downfall, after dozens of allegations of sexual assault and discrimination against him finally made their way into the public consciousness. These accusations surprised some people, because the celebrity chef in question had fashioned his public persona around being a jovial dork with a penchant for neon clogs and an air of inoffensiveness that made grandmas all over the world tune into his cooking show for over a decade. As anyone who has ever worked for him or met him can tell you, this public persona ends precisely the moment the door closes behind you. The only time I ever met this person while I worked in food media, he commented, within minutes, on the length of my dress and how easy it would be to remove it.

One of the many insidious things about men who are seemingly addicted to violating the boundaries of those they think are beneath them, is that the tendrils of that abuse reach out well past the walls of the kitchen. They diminish the hard work of the people who made that incredible food, of the people who took such great care in serving it, of the kindness of the person at the host stand, of the greatness of that glass of wine, and of the spectacular memories we have of a great meal in a beautiful place. Instead of letting a predator blot this memory out by being involved, let's blot him out instead, and pay a dutiful and hearty thanks to the people who worked in that restaurant during those times, who made and served that delicious, special food under ugly circumstances, who had to do the infuriating unpaid labor of sheltering their patrons from the abuse they were subjected to and witness to. I hope they can get some peace, and I hope he fades into poor, lonely obscurity where he belongs.

This is not the first special meal I remember — far from it — but it might be the first meal I remember knowing was special while it was happening, and that it was something I wanted to figure out how to replicate. It's the first time I recall considering *why* the meal was special, where the food came from, and why it felt so different.

I've eaten better in Ali and Mitch's company than almost anywhere else in the world, and the kitchen in their apartment has been no exception. In the 90s, Mitch occasionally took a break from getting high to cook in a kitchen or two and is probably the first veteran of a commercial kitchen I ever spent any real time with. I've learned a whole host of lessons leaning against the wall in their kitchen, and even helped to make the food a few times when I'm allowed.

I've watched Mitch turn out some truly inspired food from the galley kitchen of their Lower East Side apartment, while whichever beloved cat weaves her way around his ankles. He loves gadgetry, but not to an embarrassing degree, and he fetishizes specialty ingredients in a way that only someone who really misses California can. Ali, who wins the bread and has about as much interest in cooking the food or stirring the drinks as Mitch does in going to an office every day, has remained his most stalwart culinary devotee, his most thorough restaurant critic, his Significant Eater, to borrow his own words. I've learned a lot about love, and gender roles, and living with intention instead of obligation from these two people. They're the first people I ever knew who decided not to procreate on purpose — their reasons are not mine to share here, but what I can say is that it's allowed them to travel freely, use their expendable income on what they wish, to live as voluptuaries, unapologetically. I've always admired them for it, and especially at this point in my life, I find it hard to imagine living any other way.

In Ali and Mitch's kitchen, I've learned that you can get the best ingredients in the world, but if you don't know what you're doing with them, they simply won't taste their best. I've learned that you should try really hard to make friends with a butcher. I've learned that fresh lemon juice is the key to everything from keeping artichokes pretty to making raw Brussels sprouts become a salad. I've learned that proper cocktails are three ounces so that you can try more of them. And I've learned that you never, ever serve someone a cocktail without something to snack on — even if it's a few peanuts and a slice of salami — because we're neither barbarians nor babysitters.

Some years later, when I was allowed to drink real cocktails and not just the occasional glass of wine, Mitch asked what I'd like to drink.

"I'm not a fan of the brown liquors," I said, in a terrible moment of foreshadowing for my future proclivities, "but I'm up for just about anything else."

It must have been spring, because Mitch rolled his eyes only slightly and made me my first Aviation.

The Aviation Cocktail

Some people say this cocktail tastes like a mouthful of flowers. If that thought excites you, this is for you. If it repels you, move along, as there is no convincing you into this one. Celebrate spring some other way.

2.5 oz gin
½ oz lemon juice (squeeze it fresh or GTFO)
1.5 bar spoons Maraschino Liqueur (I use Luxardo)
1 bar spoon Crème Yvette or crème de violette
Lemon twist or brandied cherry to garnish

Add all ingredients except the garnish into a cocktail shaker and fill with cracked ice. Shake until the outside of the shaker gets frosty, at least ten seconds longer than you think. Strain into a chilled coupe, garnish with lemon twist or cherry — or both if you're feeling saucy and you can be bothered.

Makes one cocktail (you can double it, but don't make more than 2 cocktails in the shaker at once).

Albuquerque: Pasta Fazool

It's hard to think about you without being too self-deprecating.

When I do think about you, which is rarer than I ever thought it would be, I mostly think about you in your mom's — Tanya's — kitchen. That's the place where you were most reliably being nice to someone, whether it was her or me. I still remember the phone number to the white, corded phone that sat on the counter, and I think about how crazy it is that this was my only means of communicating with you then. Neither of us had a cell phone yet, and texting had barely been invented, and if we'd had Instagram back then, I would have stalked yours so hard my eyeballs would have fallen out.

I think about sitting on the floor of the pantry together picking out ramen flavors. I think about kissing in the doorway. I think about the time you made us dinner for Valentine's Day (almost certainly Tanya's work, disguised as yours) — I was wearing some stupid sexy lace thingy, but I wanted it to be a surprise, so I had a huge sweater over it, and I was so hot during dinner I thought I might die. After we ate, when I finally took it off to reveal the black, lace, off-the-shoulder thing that was underneath, you laughed.

"I wondered why you were wearing something so conservative," you said, just before you gave me the only thing I really wanted, which was your undivided attention without your clothes on.

I think about the first time I watched your mom make pasta e fagioli, pronounced "pasta fazool" in your house, because you were so obsessed with the Sicilian part of your ancestry, and whatever false mob prince confidence it gave you. I think about how she used bacon grease instead of olive oil because she was from the South, and how you made sure I was paying attention so I would know how to make it correctly, in whatever imaginary future you were convincing us both we were going to have — always with angel hair pasta, for some reason. I think about how hard you mocked me for never having eaten it before, and not knowing how to pronounce it your way, when really it should have been you who was getting mocked because you wouldn't even let your mom put an onion in it.

You had a lot of food rules: never an onion, only occasionally garlic, almost nothing white — no sour cream, rarely cheese, *NO MAYONNAISE EVER*, no visible egg whites, not too much cream. Usually, I found this to be entertaining, because I was addicted to your company, and I would end up enduring a lot worse to keep it. I watched you throw a Taco Bell burrito out the window of your car because you found an onion in it. Once, during your love affair with chicken tikka masala at the Indian restaurant near the mall, I tried to explain to you that you were actively eating onions and enjoying them because they are foundational to flavor in almost every cuisine, and it was just that you couldn't see them because they'd been pureed, and you stopped me short, "Please, Rebecca, don't ruin this for me. You have to stop."

Your mom was really the only one you wanted to make your food. There's plenty to regret about the way we parted, but one of the biggest ones I have is that I didn't ever get to see her again. She was one of the kindest people I've ever met, and I hope you're taking care of her.

I loved her laugh so much. She cried easily, when things were sad, or beautiful, and you always hugged her while you made fun of her for it. Sometimes she'd wake up in the middle of the night screaming, because she was scared someone was in the house, and we'd hear your dad gently repeat that everything was okay, and she was safe until she drifted off again. I think about the blonde ponytail falls that hung around her vanity, and about the houseplants surrounding her enormous, sunken bathtub that felt like an obscene luxury. I guess it was your dad's bathtub too, but let's be honest, that bathroom belonged to her. I think about her king-sized bed, with the gold filigree bed frame. I think about reading recipes in the newspaper in bed with her sometimes after I'd stayed the night in your bed. Something that never made sense to me was why we were allowed to do that, since you all were so obsessed with God and what he expected of you. Your faith was the most frustrating thing to me, not because of the way it limited you and separated us, but because of how smart, empathetic, and generous it actually showed you all could be. But if we're being honest, Tanya loved you even more than Jesus, and you were allowed to get away with so much.

Why did we all let you get away with so much?

Thinking of Tanya's bed makes me think of our first date. It was Halloween and we carved a pumpkin on the kitchen floor, and I showed you how to roast the seeds. You drove us around the neighborhood in your bright red Mazda RX7, taking turns unnecessarily fast, listening to Shaggy explain that "It wasn't me" on the radio. You asked what I liked to do for fun, and I said that I mostly liked to party with my friends, and you laughed because it was such a silly thing to say, but it still felt like you thought I was pretty, so it didn't hurt. I'd never held the attention of someone so beautiful and confident before, and I probably would have done anything to keep it.

I was wearing these absurd vinyl snakeskin pants, and a low-cut cashmere sweater with a little bow on it, like some stupid little millennial Lolita, and I remember thinking that I could be whoever I wanted to be with you, because you didn't go to my school and didn't know that I ate lunch in the gifted hallway with my goth friends and had never fucked anyone before.

We sat on your living room couch and talked about something I don't remember now, but I do remember when you grabbed me by the hand and pulled me onto your lap to kiss me. I remember you giving me a piggyback ride into your parents' bedroom and laying me down on that huge bed so tenderly. I told you I was nervous, that I still hadn't lost my virginity, not because I was a prude, but because I hadn't met anyone who'd made me want to. You let me climb on top of you and kiss you, and you only unzipped my pants, but didn't take them off, so I could grind against what I would discover another day was the biggest cock I'd ever seen, until I laid my head, gasping, against your neck. That's the first orgasm I ever had with another person, and when I think about this day, I always think about how you never pressured me to fuck you that afternoon, or even blow you, or reciprocate that pleasure in any way. You simply carried me back into the kitchen, ate some pumpkin seeds with me and smiled, before sending me back out into the world hearing swelling orchestra music, skin tingling, alert to a new kind of hunger. We referred to making out as "carving pumpkins" for years afterward.

God, this is a good memory. It's one of the few. It's also impossible to think about that day without thinking about the day after.

You told me to come see you after school, and I obeyed like the already lovesick puppy I was, expecting that afternoon to contain the magical, invisible fireworks that had exploded in my belly the day before. But you had a friend there, a boy your age, and I felt so young and ill-equipped, and you wouldn't really make eye-contact with me. I hung out with the two of you in the living room for a few minutes, before you announced that you two were going skating, and I should leave, sending me out the door without so much as a kiss on the cheek.

The thing about fireworks is that they never last. No one ever looks up at them in the sky and thinks, "finally — something I can count on."

I walked down the driveway, out to my own little red car in the cul-de-sac with tears forming in my eyes. I shouldn't have worn this outfit, I should have had my hair down, I should have said I was busy, I did something uncool, I could have made a choice that would have made you be nicer to me — this, of course, would become a common refrain in the years that followed. But by the time I unlocked the car door, you'd bounded out of the house, down the driveway, your limbs too long to be that graceful, spun me around with one hand behind my neck, one hand under my shirt on the small of my back, and kissed me.

"Want to carve another pumpkin tomorrow?"

How did I ride this rollercoaster for so long? It's stupid that you get to be in this book at all.

I wish I knew then what I know now about attachment styles, gaslighting, and my own worth. I wish I knew how to tell you what I wanted, and I wish I knew what I deserved. In the end, it might not have mattered. I might still have let you get away with all the myriad, creative ways you found to break my heart. I might still have gotten back together with you after you hooked up with one of my best friends and told her you wanted her to be "the last woman to ever kiss your lips." I might still have followed you to the skate park a hundred times. I might still have gone on that awful trip to Mexico with you, and the one after that, when you asked me to marry you on a balcony by the sea and I said, without being able to stop myself, "Are you sure?"

When I think back on the years we spent together, I can't remember a single meal I cooked for you. That is so unfathomable to me, because making food is how I show people I love them, and I did love you so very much. You definitely always knew you were going to hurt me, so maybe you didn't want me to show you just how much. I hope that if I met you tomorrow, instead of 22 years ago, you'd tell me you hated onions and I'd never call you again.

Albuquerque: Do Not Eat Jell-O Shots, Little Girls

Do not eat Jell-O shots, little girls, because they are not food.

Do not eat Jell-O shots because they are full of sugar and will make people think a jackhammer is trying to escape their brain tomorrow.

I will not enjoy Jell-O shots because they make me feel like a kid and an adult at the same time, even though, right now today as I eat them at a party in my friend's parents' kitchen, I am neither, and there is no part of life we get less preparation and less advice for than this one.

This one in which I am such a big fan of Jell-O shots.

This one in which I am sad because someone who isn't a boy but also isn't a man doesn't look back at me the way I look at him, even though I see him look at other people who are not girls but still aren't women all the time, right in front of my face.

This one in which I decide to let my hair be curly for the party instead of straightening it, because I want people to understand that I am feeling wild today.

This one in which I put on a leopard print halter top that I love but will never want to wear again after tonight and the Jell-O shots.

I will not choose Jell-O shots by color, rather than flavor, just because I think it's fun and funny to say how much I like the taste of "blue."

I will not use someone else's finger, someone whose nickname is Booger, to release my Jell-O shot from its plastic condiment container, swallow it while I make eye contact with him, and then put his fingers in my mouth to suck the rest of the Jell-O off.

I will not eat Jell-O shots, girls, then open my eyes to find that I am kissing one person, someone whose nickname is Booger, while someone else, someone I don't even want to suck Jell-O from the fingers of, has penetrated me from behind.

When I panic because I did not consent to this, but also don't know how I got into that room on that bed, or how to get out of it without making everyone very upset, I'll reach behind my own ass to make sure that there is at least a condom present between me and this person I do not like and did not ask to be there, and when I feel the latex there, I will breathe a sigh of exquisitely inadequate relief.

When I panic the next day that everyone will think I wanted to do this thing I did not ask to do, I'll blame myself, the halter top, the blue Jell-O shots and the curls in my hair.

I will keep it a secret from everyone.

Later, when I am a woman, and feel very far away from this day, I'll read my journal entry from the day after Booger and his friend double-teamed me without my consent, and I will feel so sad that I registered this as a personal moral failure, which it wasn't, rather than as sexual assault, which it was.

I'll know then, when I am a woman feeling sad, that it wasn't Jell-O's fault.

I'll even know that it wasn't my fault, it wasn't my friend's fault for having the party, for making the blue Jell-O shots, for having the spare bedroom.

It was Booger's fault, and Booger's friend's fault, and their faults alone.

I will never see them again.

I will learn to like the taste of blue again.

I will go to other parties and fuck people on purpose.

I will learn that letting my hair be wild is not a dangerous decision.

I will learn that I am supposed to make everyone very upset when they violate my boundaries and my body.

I will never wear the leopard print halter top again.

Albuquerque: Getting the Coffee

The day we knew my dad was going to die, I had to pick up the coffee.

Saying it that way might indicate a kind of callousness on my family's part, but really it was a matter of both convenience and the fact that there is very little that my family is capable of doing before they've had coffee. Taking one of their most beloved brothers / sons / husbands / fathers off life support is definitely not within the realm of the possible without significant caffeine intake.

It sounds ridiculous now, as if we're talking about attending an SAT prep class or filling out a W-2 form, but that day, getting the coffee seemed to be very important.

Unlike the rest of the family who were a solid 20 minutes away, Sean and I lived a mere five minute drive from the hospital where my father had spent the last week of his life. Although we hadn't realized at the beginning of that week that "last" would mean both prior and final, that day it had finally become clear as crystal — this was the end.

Sometimes I feel envious when I hear stories from people whose loved ones die of drawn-out disease. That's a fucked up thing to say, but I had to tell you the truth, because that's what we're doing here. There's the same terrible, inevitable march to the end, sometimes spread out over excruciating months and years, but at least there's time to say the things you want to, for them to tell you the things they want to, an opportunity to know how that person whose opinion has always mattered most to you feels about their mortality, about their life as a nearly complete story. I imagine that my father, staring down into the most unknown depths of his life, would have found a way to make us all feel at peace with it. He would have had some terribly dark and hilarious joke, he would have looked at our faces and reminded us that he'd already given us the tools to be okay — and probably to be great.

The truth is that he could have been trying to, which is one of the scariest things to admit about taking someone with an anoxic brain injury off life support — you kind of don't know what's going on in there. He could have been, his body out of his control, trying endlessly to find a way to communicate to us that he was still in there, that he would make it through this, and that we should all just calm down and keep our hands away from the switch. Almost certainly not, as the doctors assured us, but I know it didn't stop my brother and me from having nightmares for years that it was true.

In our defense, our dad gave us some signs that this might be the case during that week. After the operation that cleared his aorta of the insidious stuff that was blocking it to begin with — that made him collapse, retching in the living room where my mother found him — the doctors said his heart was beating stronger than they would have ever expected. His heart had been saved, they told us, allowing us a brief moment of respite from the marathon of muscle-clenching terror we'd been engaged in. Now the problem, they said, with that terrible intonation that indicates you should pay attention to this part, was his brain. Without knowing how long he'd been without oxygen during his heart attack, there was no way to know how his brain function had been affected. I will never forget the folksy, apologetic way the doctor explained, "The brain sure does like it's oxygen, ya know?"

In the years since, I've come to understand that surviving an acute myocardial infarction anywhere outside of a hospital setting is exceedingly rare, no matter how diligent and earnest the CPR, no matter how beloved the victim, no matter how hard you wish that statistic wasn't true.

We gave him every test we could think of that week – EKGs, ECGs, CT scans – but also, we talked to him, held his hands, asked him questions we were sure would provoke a response in that formidable cavern that once quizzed us on spelling bee words and political ideologies. One of us, I can tell you, punched him square in the arm as hard as I could and told him to snap the fuck out of it. We were almost sure that he wasn't in there anymore, that whatever magic connected his brain tissue in the way that made him *him* had been strangled out. And then someone held a clementine under his nose and his eyes shot open.

I mean they SHOT open, like someone had just woke him up from a nap (which is something that all during his life would have required us drawing the short straw to attempt). This made all the logical sense in the world. Food had been the answer to most questions in my life, why not this one? Someone grabbed a bowl of green chile stew and held it there, inches from his face – it elicited the same reaction. This was progress, we just knew it. My mother, overcome with excitement and relief ran to his side and looked right into his now saucer-like eyes, "I know you're scared and probably have a lot of questions," she said blinking back tears, "But there are people here taking care of you and everything's going to be okay." To think back on it now, I swear he looked relieved. I'm sure there's a medical term for what was occurring as his eyes slowly closed again, and he drifted off to what we all really hoped was a well-deserved nap, leaving us once again with only the beeps and boops of the medical equipment keeping him alive.

I thought a lot that week about how hard this must have been on the doctors. How it must break their hearts every day to see people hope so hard they pass out in uncomfortable chairs next to the hospital beds of their loved ones. How impossible it must be to watch someone hold a clementine under their clinically brain-dead brother's nose and diagnose the effects as a miracle rather than a highly surprising manifestation of some of our most basic lower brain functions. After the clementine incident, my aunt Ali turned to me and wondered aloud if we were all clinging to false hope. "Maybe," I said. "But even if we are, is there a more worthwhile time to be optimistic?"

We agreed there wasn't, since, if we were wrong, we'd be devastated either way. We were wrong, as we'd suspected all along, and we were fucking devastated, as we'd expected all along.

As Sean and I walked from the car to the Starbucks, I considered just sitting down in the parking lot. Maybe a good, old-fashioned protest would delay things a little longer. But my legs kept moving me along, through the frigid parking lot and into the smooth-jazz-filled Starbucks that had been filling us with acrid caffeine all week. As we approached the counter, the person who had been working the early morning shift each day was there. They, no doubt, recognized our sallow, underfed, under-rested faces from other days that week, and probably assumed that we'd been lugging boxes of coffee each day to some grad school study sessions at the nearby university — not momentarily taking the edge off for an entire family of displaced, neurotic assholes clinging to their last bits of hope.

"Good morning!" they sang.

"Good morning," I said.

"How are you today?" they asked.

In my mind I stood there for hours trying to figure out what to say. I was terrible. I expected this to actually be the worst day of my life to date. I wanted a time machine. I wanted to go back to a week before that moment and try to stop this from happening. I was sadder, more scared and more confused than I'd ever been. I wondered how many times this person, or any of us for that matter, had asked someone how their day was going on the worst day of their life without realizing it. I was angry with them for not knowing any better, then instantly felt guilty for judging them, when all they wanted was to make polite conversation on an early December day in fucking Albuquerque. I realized that I was going to have to start remembering the last moments — the last time I hugged my dad, the last thing he said to me, the last time I saw him before he was in a hospital bed. I wondered what would happen if I told her all this and then promptly vomited on the counter like I wanted to.

"I'm fine, thank you. How are you?"

That's what I said. It's probably what you would have said too, under the same circumstances, unless you are a total sociopath. If this experience taught me nothing else, it's that I really fucking care about customer service, both on the giving and receiving end. My dad would have laughed at that joke, even if you didn't.

We ordered our box of coffee, forewent pastries because it didn't really seem like an appropriate morning to go full Continental, and paid.

"You guys have a great day," the counter person said.

"Thank you, and do the same."

We again traveled the seemingly endless expanse of the parking lot and sat down in the car like we weighed 40 tons. Sean looked at me like he looks at me when he knows my brain is about to absolutely explode and said, "How are you today?" the way any good Starbucks employee would.

"I'm headed up the street to take my father off life support. How the fuck are you?"

"Feel better?"

"Yep. Thanks."

He started the car, and we brought the coffee.

There are some moments too private to share, even for me. Attempting to describe the hours in that ICU room between the decision and the last time he breathed feels like holding my hand in a fire. But I return often to the moments afterward, when we gathered our things, his things, and walked out of the hospital, pushing a wheeled cart full of floral arrangements through the automatic doors in the lobby and into the cold afternoon air. I remember thinking to myself how easily we could be mistaken for a family celebrating a birth, a recovery, a victory. There were upwards of 20 bouquets on that cart, one with a balloon that said GET WELL SOON in a cheerful chartreuse. I hated that balloon. I hated those floral arrangements. And I still can't stand the smell of stargazer lilies.

But I wasn't crying anymore. I was too tired.

However morbid, it feels good to remember that week in the hospital. It's like worrying a canker sore — the sensation isn't pleasant, but it is familiar and endlessly tempting. I guess it feels good to think about that awful week and the details therein because at least then my dad was technically alive. Somehow the whole family was gathered there again, at Presbyterian Hospital, looking weird in a waiting room during a Jewish holiday spent in the hospital — this time lighting the Hanukkah menorah and (this is macabre) playing dreidel while we waited to see if our dad would wake up. I hadn't yet learned all the things I didn't want to know about the way my family deals with grief, about the ways we'd come apart, about just how durable a social and emotional glue my father quietly was for us. There were times when we had some hope, and times when we held each other together, there were times when we disagreed, had to walk away from conversations, but at least his brain was in the next room, dimly lit as it may have been.

Thinking about the weeks, months, years after the fact feels worse. We've all made some regrettable decisions, some difficult choices, said the wrong thing, melted into puddles in front of one another. Writing now, 14 years later, I could still very easily become a puddle.

But I guess there's a lot to learn in a meltdown. And what I learned the following week is that you need to own at least one non-stick pan.

Waking up the morning after he died was one of the most disorienting experiences of my life. Whenever your world shifts enormously, there's a moment between opening your eyes and remembering reality, a liminal space where you're present, but reality is far away, can be held at bay. A brief moment of magical thinking, to borrow a phrase from Joan Didion. There wasn't much sleep during the week prior — I was always ready to get the call we were all dreading: that it had happened, that it would happen, that it was time. After he was gone, there was nothing left to be afraid of. We were all exhausted, and I slept like a rock. I woke up to the sun shining in the window and that half a second between me and the world, but it only lasted as long as an inhale. By the exhale it all rushed back in, and I had to get out of bed without a dad for the first time.

I tend to find my way back to myself by cooking something. It focuses me, centers me, calms me down. But forcing it rarely works, and there was so much food already.

Almost a decade later, I heard Julia Reed speak at a food writing conference in Knoxville, Tennessee. Reed's food writing is singular and wonderful, but this time she told a particular story that I haven't been able to forget. Her own grandparents died in a tragic accident. When her family received the call, the motions of preparing for what would come next began immediately. As her mother rushed out the door to make funeral arrangements, she shouted back to Reed with all the importance in the universe, "Go clean out the refrigerator!"

In the American South, your refrigerator will immediately fill up with Jell-O salads, potato salads, deviled eggs, and fried chicken. In Utah, you can count on at least three versions of funeral potatoes. In Brooklyn, you should prepare your freezer for gallons and gallons of red sauce. If your dad dies in New Mexico, like mine did, there will be tamales, enchiladas, green chile stew, and a lot of tortillas. But what I really remember was the baked ziti. I have no idea who made this baked ziti, or if I even knew them particularly well. I remember that it was in an aluminum catering pan, covered in tin foil, and that the layer of mozzarella on top of it was about an inch thick. Over the next few days, I ate that baked ziti for breakfast, lunch, dinner and snacks in between. I don't know if anyone else got any of it. But anytime someone who I know or love loses someone, that is the dish I'm inclined to make.

It seemed impossible that days would continue to occur after we lost him. Not that I couldn't bear to go on, it just seemed kind of physically impossible that the world would continue to exist as we'd known it. Like the void of his weight would tip gravity out of alignment. One of the hardest things to process about grief is that it's all your own, even when you're experiencing it concurrently with other people, even when your grief has the same source.

But eventually, a week had passed. We'd had a funeral. I'd given a eulogy. We'd eaten the funeral food. We'd washed dishes, done laundry, paid the rent. We were expected to return to work. It all just kept going.

In a moment of resolution, I woke up one morning and decided to make us breakfast. "You've eaten all the baked ziti. Now, how about an over-easy egg," I thought to myself. I probably sauteed some vegetables to go underneath — another one of my ritual urges when I feel like my life is out of control — just eat a vegetable and something will feel better. I pulled out a frying pan, the one we always used for eggs, melted some butter into it, cracked an egg. I salted it, let it set up, until the whites just started to ruffle and dance around at the edges. I grabbed a spatula and slid it under the egg to flip it. It stuck. The yolk broke and spilled out across the frying pan.

Fuck. Let's try that one more time.

I could feel rage fluttering near the back of my throat. Melted some butter in the pan. Just one simple task. Cracked an egg. I just need to complete one simple task. Salted it. Just to feed us, and then we'll feel better. Let it set up. You can't control everything; you can't be scared of everything. The whites started to ruffle and dance around the edges. This is how you start to feel okay. I slid the spatula under the egg to flip it. You need to start to feel okay. It stuck. Fuck. The yolk broke and spilled out across the frying pan. And then I was sitting on the floor sobbing with a frying pan full of egg yolk in the garbage can.

In an instant, Sean was there on the floor with me. I was embarrassed — this was not my first fried egg, nor my first crying fit, nor my first mundane task gone awry. Everything just felt so much harder than usual. I wondered how long I was going to feel so unraveled. It felt terribly maudlin, and I couldn't stop crying.

He looked at me like he looks at me when he knows my brain is about to absolutely explode and said, "I'll order us a non-stick pan."

So much of this story is about how good he is.

Albuquerque: Thin Air

Anyone can land a plane at sea level. Which is something I forget consistently, until I'm roughly 15,000 feet above Albuquerque in an airplane that is rapidly nosing downward, then re-pressurizing up, up, riding the rolling waves of air that undulate around the Sandias — the 10,000-foot mountain range that anchor my hometown to the east.

Albuquerque sits at 2,600 feet above sea level, which means that the air is thinner there. In Boston, or New Orleans, or the Caribbean (even with their harrowingly short runways), the air is appropriately thick. It wants to help the airplane stop. Up there, where the air is thin and the jet stream is unpredictable, pilots have to know that the vessel they're piloting will take three times the distance, effort, and skill to slow to a stop. Up there, the air doesn't care if your plane stops. It's busy licking new caverns into limestone and tanning coyote hides.

This is where I'm from.

I impressed myself (and probably no one else) on my last visit home when I managed to finally articulate something I'd been trying to say about my home state, ever since the first time I returned from living somewhere else.

"I feel very connected to this place," I repeated again and again, "but I've never felt *of* this place."

New Mexico is strange in a way that's hard to explain to someone until they see it. If you've never seen a cruise ship before, it's hard to explain how small you will feel standing next to one, and how alienating it is to stare up at the towering thickness of cold steel, still where boats are usually in motion. The desert is like this too. You can describe how much bigger the sky is there, how much wider the highways are, and how much thinner the air feels, but it's all just talk until you're actually hurtling down I-25, with the red hills, purple mountains, green piñons, and blue sky staring back at you, unmoved by your relative, tiny existence.

The sky in New Mexico is so big and so accessible to the naked eye, that on days like that one in December, it was possible to feel like we were looking at multiple seasons at once. If we started with our gaze to the volcanic west, it was spring with farmland and flowers and warm sunshine. As our eyes traveled south, toward Albuquerque — the state's biggest city and the place of my birth — we saw heat rippled up from pavement and buildings, and a dark, ominous, purple-black thunderstorm brewing in the corner of the panorama. This is summer in the desert. Shifting just slightly east to the Sandias, those 10,000-foot mountains I spent my youth at the base of, the dark purple of their craggy surface gave way to white, powdery snow. We've abruptly skipped fall in this scenario, because fall is an unmistakable season impossible to replicate in New Mexico, punctuated by hot air balloons in the sky and the smell of roasting chiles in the air. It is, without question, the best.

This is all to say: It is beautiful, but it is weird as hell. And it's this dichotomy I've been struggling to understand and describe since I was old enough to care about where I wanted to make my home once I had the choice. I always knew that it wouldn't be there, but I'd never bothered to consider why not.

The answer, I suppose, if you boil it all the way down to its most primitive essence, is danger.

The desert, as it turns out, has a lot of stuff that wants to kill you. Hiking in New Mexico is a high-stakes proposition. There are scorpions, snakes, mountain lions, bears. Sometimes it's 90 degrees during the day and 30 once the sun goes down. It's easy to get dehydrated and disoriented at that altitude, even if you're experienced. And then, there are the people.

When you watch the brutality of an old Western and think, "Jesus fucking Christ," that's where I'm from. Burgundy blood and red clay and purple mountains. That's where I'm from.

Yes, *Breaking Bad* takes place where I'm from, and although I spent years reminding people that it is a work of fiction, once I finally watched it, I recognized the motels I went to school down the street from, the old Victorian house downtown where I often got drunk underage, and the scary and familiar feeling of poverty, addiction, and desperation mixed like sand in the air.

I dream of my parents' house often — usually I'm trying to lock all the doors in anticipation of a home invasion. It is situated on the corner of a wide, quiet street in a neighborhood frequently referred to by locals as "The Northeast Whites," because they (The Northeast Heights) are predominantly just that. People think of it as a "nice neighborhood" (the implications of which are a little too obvious, given its nickname). Even still, it is Albuquerque, and there have been bars on all the windows that aren't visible from the street since we moved there as a family when I was 11. Once, a few years after my dad died, someone broke in through the sliding glass back door, crept into my mother's room and stole most of her grandmother's heirloom jewelry while she was painting silk in her studio two bedrooms away. It's an easy place to feel unsettled.

"It's weird to be back," my brother said. "Because nothing has really changed."

"And the things that have changed aren't welcome additions," I said. "Like, oh —"

"— that's a Wal-Mart now," we said in unison, about what used to be our favorite local bookstore.

We were about to spend the anniversary of my dad's death in our parents' house together for the first time since the thing itself occurred 14 years prior. Jason was 16 when it happened, and I was 23, and now we were both grown adults with partners, and jobs, and our own universes being delicately suspended while we drove through the desert to get everyone breakfast burritos. I expected the melancholy. I expected the fatigue. But I didn't really expect how frustrating it would be.

The linoleum in my mother's kitchen is peeling up where the heater blows over it. There are empty tomato sauce jars filling every spare cupboard space, saved to use for storage. Some of them have been there since I lived there last, somewhere around 2005. The cookbooks are piled in exactly the same stack, leaning in the same direction, threatening to fall onto the floor in exactly the same way. There are a few additions, mostly things that I have sent her to try to feel some camaraderie, since food is usually where we find it.

She still has the same knife block as when we were kids, the same sugar bowl, the same coffee maker my dad last used the morning he had a heart attack. His mugs sit in the cabinet like a shrine — I like the one with the line drawing of the cat on it best, one of his favorites despite our always having been a dog family. My mother doesn't use those, though. She uses the turquoise Fiestaware mugs, in a shape and size that the company no longer makes. They are so stained with the Darjeeling tea-water she microwaves for herself every day — mostly half-and-half with a splash of black tea — that no matter how hard you scrub them, you can't get the rings out.

The sink faucet needs to be replaced. There are house plants without enough soil, all lining the sink. There too, I found empty soap bottles, a pile of used sponges, a lunch box I used in middle school, the same plastic cutting boards I used when I came home from school for a snack. I know that some of these things are my responsibility to help her resolve, but I don't know where to start. For someone who is so good at asking people to help her do things, I wonder how she's never made friends with a plumber.

Whenever it goes too far — like when I open the drawer under the oven and realize it is filled exclusively with old mail — I bring up the idea of getting rid of some clutter, and she responds the same way, "Well, *you're* very good at that."

I'm not, I think to myself, *I just don't want it to turn into this.*

"Well, *you're* very good at that" is deployed both as a compliment and an insult. It's a thank you for the all the visits we've spent clearing out the garage, doing runs to Goodwill, turning my old bedroom into a guest room instead of a shrine to my dead father's things and my childhood doll collection. But it's also a castigation — for not being sentimental enough, for not being patient enough, for leaving her behind when she needed help.

My brother tries his best. He takes the trash out. He plays Animal Crossing in the living room with his girlfriend. He sighs and smiles wistfully when we catch each other's eyes like *The Office*'s Jim Halpert to the camera. Occasionally, when my mom complains about something easily fixable for the 40th time, he will break, take a sharp breath in, and just say gently, "Ok, what should we do about it?"

When she walks from room to room narrating what she's doing aloud, I try to remind myself that she's lived alone for 14 years after really never *being* alone for her entire adult life. That these ticks are survival instincts. That she's been keeping herself company all this time, and that she probably begrudges us for that.

These days, mostly what I learn in my mother's kitchen is how different we are. Or maybe it's where I recognize the difficult ways in which we are the same — like how on Hanukkah she wanted help frying the latkes, but then stood there critiquing how I was doing it the entire time.

There are plenty of things we agree on, like the fact that the skin on chocolate pudding is the whole point. And that you can go to the trouble of whipping heavy cream to put on top of it if you want, but first you should try pouring a few spoonfuls of cream right onto the pudding itself, letting a little run onto your spoon with each bite. We agree that Mollie Katzen is a living vegetable goddess, that there's no point to making a small brisket, and that having your friends for dinner is one of the best parts of being alive.

My mother has taught me the kinds of cooking lessons that you don't soon forget. Always cook with wine that you'd like to drink, because you probably will be while you're cooking with it. Always be ready to put out a snack before dinner. If you see two recipes you like across the page from each other, smash them together and see what happens — this is how her legendary Green Soup came about: an almost-vichyssoise that has become a staple in our house, that I've written about so many times I lost track of all of them.

Sue's Green Soup

adapted from the *Pop+Dutch Snackbook, Vol. 1*

2 Tbsp. butter
4 cups cucumber, peeled and diced
2 potatoes, peeled and sliced
1 bunch of scallions, sliced
2 leeks, sliced and very thoroughly rinsed
1 bunch of fresh spinach, chopped
3 cups chicken stock
½ a lemon, juiced
1 cup half and half
2 cups buttermilk
Salt and pepper to taste

Heat butter in a heavy-bottomed stockpot over medium heat. Sauté scallions and leeks in the butter until soft. Add chicken stock, cucumbers, potatoes, salt and pepper, and lemon, and bring to a boil. (I know that it sounds crazy to cook a cucumber into soup, but I just want you to trust me and trust Sue Orchant. This is the secret to making this soup verdant and special, and somehow refreshing and comforting at the same time.) Reduce the heat, and simmer uncovered until potatoes are soft. Add spinach and cook for 2 — 3 minutes, until wilted but still bright green.

Remove the pot from the heat. If you have an immersion blender, blend the soup up right in the pot, until it's very smooth. If not, transfer the soup carefully in batches to a blender and puree. Return the soup to the pot, or into a large bowl.

Add buttermilk and half and half. Taste for seasoning. Serve immediately or chill and serve cold.

Serves 4 — 6

This is the kitchen where I, historically, have learned the most.

It's where I first made pain au chocolat from scratch after I got dumped, just for myself. It's where my mom taught me to pound chicken breasts between two pieces of wax paper before coating them in flour, egg, and breadcrumbs, and pan-frying them in butter. It's where I watched my dad "be in charge of the steak," marinating supermarket ribeyes in teriyaki sauce and lemon pepper before grilling them to a perfect medium-rare almost every time. He was also in charge of making the stir-fry, which he did in an enormous carbon-steel wok, each ingredient already prepped and ready to be added in the proper order in rapid succession.

"It has to be so hot that it makes you nervous," he explained, with a little grin, six-foot-three and improbably light on his feet.

Once, on a morning before summer art classes we were taking at a prep school that neither one of us could get into but were allowed to attend because my mom was teaching there, my brother sat at the kitchen table while I absentmindedly popped green grapes into my mouth directly from the crisper drawer. I stood up, closed the fridge, and made eye contact with Jason while I realized that one of the grapes had lodged itself whole, right on top of my windpipe — that I couldn't breathe or make a sound, that I was choking.

"Mom," he yelled with an unbelievable casualness, "something's wrong with Becca."

I stood there, frozen, wondering if this would really be how I went out. I'd imagined a host of disasters in my little brain, but somehow asphyxiation by fruit had never crossed my mind. My mother ran into the room, pointed me toward the sink, executed the Heimlich maneuver with a practiced fluidity that surprised me, and shot the whole grape directly into the garbage disposal.

"Are you okay, sweetie?" she asked.

"I think so," I said.

"Good," she said, "we have to go."

That kitchen doesn't feel like mine anymore, because it isn't. My mom has spent the last 14 years making it her own, and so although I balk when I realize that she still has one of Jason's baby spoons in the utensil drawer, I leave it there, even though I want to throw it away; to make room, to purge, to de-clutter this space of its nostalgia.

"I actually have a good reason for that one," she explains. "It's the only one that fits into the skinny jar of capers."

My brother and I laughed and shrugged at this one, having to admit it was a great call and that we had to hand it to her.

The night before my dad's anniversary, our mom clasped her hands together in front of her heart and told us she had a ritual on this night, and that she wanted us to participate. She asked us to put on a particular Grateful Dead record, and dug a yahrzeit candle out of the pantry. She set it on a turquoise Fiestaware saucer on the kitchen counter, next to a picture of my dad, mustached and grinning as he always was for our entire lives. She lit the candle, asked my brother and I to recite the Mourner's Kaddish with her – which we did while our gentile partners looked on in bewilderment. It was so intimate and private that it was almost impossible to live through without cracking a joke to break the tension, but somehow, we held it together, and collectively exhaled with relief once it was over and we could drink, play a game, get back to normal life outside the searing vulnerability of a grief somehow so distant and so close at the same time.

Sean and I slept in my old bedroom, situated between my mom in hers, and Jason and his girlfriend on an air mattress on the floor of his old bedroom – a full house for the first time in a long time. My mom has always been an incredibly light sleeper, who stirs at the sound of feet tiptoeing across carpet. The bathroom across the hallway from my bedroom has a door that squeaks like you're stepping on a cat. So, when I stirred from restless sleep on a sagging double mattress meant to hold one teenager and not two whole adults, I wandered across the dark house, through the den, through the kitchen, to pee in the half-bathroom in the laundry room instead. This bathroom has a sliding pocket door and its own heating vent. I forget when I'm not home, but this little windowless room has often been a haven for me when I need some space in this house where solitary time has been a rare commodity. Sometimes, the air feels a little thicker in there.

Passing through the kitchen on the way to this quiet refuge, the yahrzeit candle still glowed on the counter. Sean had tried to blow it out before we went to bed, wisely valuing fire safety over tradition, like a rational person. I stopped him with urgency, explaining that it had to burn until it naturally went out, that it was "major bad juju to blow it out." I lingered there with my dad's photo and his commemorative flame, aware that it was my first time alone in the kitchen since I'd gotten home. It felt a little like I was getting to have a quiet moment with Marc, like we used to when it was morning, and the house was still dark except for the kitchen light. Still quiet except for the sound of the coffee maker gurgling. It felt peaceful, and significant, and — for me — a lot more holy than mumbling transliterated Hebrew in front of other people.

The next morning, the candle was still burning, and we missed him just as much as we always do.

Truro: A Sad Lasagna

We asked two friends if we could come to dinner — that is, if we could please pick up take-out and bring it to them. They'd recently had their second child in three years, had sold their sandwich shop the next town over, and were about to start a new business the next spring, so we figured they could use a break.

"Yes, please come. We'd love to see you. But we're making lasagna. To clarify, Claire is making lasagna," Ellery said.

Sean protested, reminding them that we were trying to make socializing labor free for them — for once — these two sweet people who host us and feed us so freely and frequently, but they insisted.

As we sat down to dinner, poured the wine, and ferried plates to the table, I thanked them again for cooking.

"You know, I had to make lasagna already, so I figured I'd just make two," Claire said.

"You *had* to make lasagna?" I asked.

"Well, it was a sad lasagna," she replied, as she negotiated a gigantic slice on a spatula.

That universal, sinking feeling that something *bad* had happened rose like steam from the meal in front of us. It turned out that one of their very young staff members had died that week, and that she had made the first lasagna for his mom.

Having known the indispensable comforts of pasta and cheese in our darkest hours, I think we appreciated it even more. And having had the awful responsibility of reporting tragedy to others before, I tried not to shy away from the topic, and asked them questions about what happened, and if they were okay. One of the most terrible weights of grief is being afraid that sharing it will ruin everyone else's day. It felt like a loss that was detached enough to make questions appropriate, but close enough that Claire's voice caught in her throat while she answered.

It was at once heartening and heartbreaking to have such an easy shorthand for tragedy; to know that we make huge portions of comfort food in aluminum catering trays for only a few reasons, joy or pain.

Manhattan: Pork Tenderloin Under the Williamsburg Bridge

It's a bitter pill that one of the most reliable shared human experiences is losing someone you love. They're the kinds of shocking despair missiles that come at you sideways, when you least expect it, while you're just trying to cook yourself dinner or celebrate with your friends.

If you count yourself among these grieving hordes, I'm so sorry, and I love you so much. The trite refrain that we all "thought we had more time with them" always rings in my ears — trite because it's so cruelly and exactly true. We always think that.

One of these tremendous losses was Marcelo Gallegos. Marcy — like all the great ones we lose way too soon, literally defies explanation. After his death, as in his life, there is nothing I could tell you that would accurately express his booming voice, his maniacal laugh, his otherworldly talent, his unbelievable gift of gab, the insane ice green of his eyes, his love of all things luxurious and decadent, and filthy and rotten.

Thinking of him today, it seems impossible that we'd get to have him for a long time, but I really wanted to be wrong about that.

Marcy and I went to Sandia High School together, where he was the first out queer I knew, glistening, in a vintage silk cravat or something, like a beacon of how you could just be yourself instead of trying to pretend to be different. I suspect he'd be repulsed and flattered in equal measure by that admission, "That's disgusting, thank you so much." He wasn't doing it on purpose, he was just being himself because he had no other choice, because his brain was wired to be exactly the spooky, creative freak he was for the entire time I knew him.

I hung around with people he was friends with in school, but we weren't close friends until we all lived in New York in 2008 — Sean and I in Brooklyn, Marcy, Topher, and Mike on the other side of the river in what you could loosely describe as a three bedroom apartment on Attorney Street, steps away from the majesty of the Williamsburg Bridge overpass. Marcy slept in what was intended, I think, to be a porch just off the living room, in a nest of vintage fabrics, an odd collection of lace and floral handkerchiefs, occasionally, and somewhat notoriously, using a doughnut as a pillow after a rowdy night.

I have so many memories of nights spent there, drinking shitty beer, watching Marcy smoke a cigarette from between Topher's toes, laughing and screaming "GIMME THAT DICK" at each other in the backyard until the neighbors complained more than once, gently fearing for our lives every time we stepped into the elevator. I remember thinking that it felt really good to be around people who loved you the most when you were at your darkest and most socially unacceptable. Anyone who ever did karaoke with Marcelo will never forget it. Certainly, none of us will ever forget the afterparty of Topher's birthday dinner, when we casually tossed an entire case of wine glasses off the roof for some reason, cheering every time one shattered in the alley — only slowing down once someone hurled a bucket of tar over the side of the building and we decided we'd gone too far. And then there were the feasts.

Once, Topher came home to Marcy hard at work on a full lobster dinner. When asked how he could have afforded all that, he responded blithely, "I got them under the Manhattan Bridge — they're like a dollar a pound down there." Dinners around the lazy Susan at Congee Village were always cause for calling in sick the next day, having consumed 20 courses and at least three bright blue cocktails. But my favorite nights were with the *Two Fat Ladies*. We all spent hours falling in love with reruns of the great British cooking series, specifically with the ladies themselves, Jennifer and Clarissa. This common love of British humor, dirty jokes and dairy products, culminated one magical night in 2011 when Marcy made us their Pork Tenderloin in Pastry — basically a pork Wellington, stuffed with ham, herbed breadcrumbs, and so, so much cream.

It will go down as one of the great meals of my life, enjoyed in a cramped kitchen on a spring night, before we all flung ourselves out into the rest of our lives across the country from each other. The "two fat ladies" truly seemed to love each other, right down to their last day together, when Jennifer passed away in 1999. Her last request was a tin of caviar. Clarissa, unable to get it to her in time, ate the whole thing herself as a tribute to her friend. When we got the news that Marcy had died, Sean and I basically did exactly that with a bottle of Cognac, hoping to follow suit.

I will miss his artwork, the tiny glimpses into the gorgeous nightmares he held in his head. I will miss his incredible mixtapes, full of music I didn't know I wanted or wasn't ready to appreciate until much later. I will miss talking with him about the under-appreciated sexual value of body odor, and for getting to chuckle at his endless lust for his friends. I'll miss the unbelievable rush of making him laugh, and the tender sweetness of watching him and Sean become friends. I will miss just knowing that he's out there, making the world weirder and queerer and more full of art. I, along with most of the people who love him, really hope he haunts us.

III.

Provincetown: They Spelled It Wrong

Although they were the namesake of our restaurant, I never got to meet Pop and Duch — and actually, even though they were Sean's great-grandparents, neither did he.

A caveat, right out of the gate: We spelled it wrong.

That's what Sean's grandmother, Lorraine said, when she came to our shop for the first and only time on our very first opening day. Lorraine, who lived to be 99, still had a freakishly sharp memory. The last time we saw her, she spent the entire visit complaining about the portion sizes of the food in her assisted living facility ("The chocolate pudding is the size of a thumbnail"); the menu choices ("I don't care for a sandwich at supper"); and pointing out which bouquets of birthday flowers in her room had been sent by whom, and how well she thought they had done, respectively.

When Lorraine crossed the threshold of Pop+Dutch that day in 2014 to deliver us a "good luck" potted gladiola, wish us well, and review our rendition of her snickerdoodle cake recipe ("It's fine"), she may have just thought we were being careless with details. The details, to be fair, were a little sparse.

According to Lorraine, when Sean and his siblings were born, she asked Pop and Duch if they'd like to meet their great-grandchildren and their response was — and I very much suspect she was paraphrasing — "Not particularly."

The story of their nicknames, as I know it, is that Duch, Lorraine's mother-in-law, was called that because she nicknamed herself "Duchess," the legend being that she preferred to wear elbow-length evening gloves whenever she could and aspired to a station higher than her own. Pop, who was actually Duch's brother, not her husband, had come back to live with her and help with the kids after she kicked their father, Erik, out of the house for too much gin, not enough patience, a hot temper, and cruel hands. As opposed to Duch's aspirations for high society, Pop — a lifelong bachelor, as the saying goes — drank Ballantine ale, was fond of tinned sardines straight from the can, and smoked Pall Malls. We have a picture of them on the lawn of their summer home in Manomet, Massachusetts, with Lorraine, then in her 20s holding both their hands, the blonde hair she still had until the day she died glimmering in the sun.

Duch very much wanted to be classy; Pop preferred to remain otherwise, and we've tried to incorporate both of their spirits into the sandwich shop and market we bestowed with their names. Both Sean and I loved the way their names sounded together, and we loved the homage to a non-traditional family in all its imperfect weirdness. We also knew that "Pop+Duch" wouldn't quite register in the public consciousness (as it was, the boys of Provincetown began referring to our shop, I like to think lovingly, as the "Poop+Douche" before our first summer was over), so we added the erroneous "t" to try to save ourselves from ridicule. We didn't realize then how many actual Dutch tourists would subsequently run into the shop expectantly, wondering who was Dutch and if we made Dutch food. We didn't set out to disappoint the people of The Netherlands, but a few have certainly left our shop crestfallen.

As anyone who has ever started a business can tell you, the spelling of the name is one of roughly 70,000 details you didn't think of when you were dreaming it up. While Sean and I walked up and down the streets of Brooklyn fantasizing about agua fresca flavors, sat in pubs poring over possible breakfast menus, and spent feverish weeks trying to time our resignations from our jobs in New York with the pending acceptance of a commercial lease in Provincetown, we didn't know we'd have to submit sign dimensions to the town to get our business license. We didn't know we'd need to become experts on what kind of flooring is easiest to install in a building that tilts constantly backward toward the bay and contains not a single right angle. We didn't know — and this one was really a bitch — how hard it is to find a plumber on Cape Cod in April.

If you've never been to Provincetown, here's what you need to know: It's one of the most beautiful, absurdly cute seaside villages I've ever been to, filled with visitors who are hell-bent on indulging every decadence they can think of. They want to eat, they want to drink, they want to fuck, they want to dance, they want to lounge on the beach, they want to buy shit with Provincetown printed on it more than you would believe. Mostly they want to be all the way themselves, which is the real reason people end up here.

There's an old saying about Cape Cod restaurants that the menu is designed for "the sixth person." The first five of them probably want a cup of chowder and a lobster roll, but what if the sixth one wants tacos? Our season here is so short, that everyone falls all over themselves to make sure they can grab as much business as possible while they're open. Some people make an entire year's-worth of money in four months. This leads to a lot of bad food, in a lot of small restaurants, with a frazzled staff and questionable quality. You can't possibly be good at *everything*. Most places, understandably, cater to what people want to eat on a day trip to Provincetown. We set out to make a sandwich shop for the rest of us. We've never sold lobster rolls, we use A LOT of vegetables, and we focus on making the best version we can of the comforts we relate to most. A great turkey sandwich, a great Italian combo, Nana's cake recipe, Mom's soup. We wanted to be the place where other service industry workers wanted to eat lunch, and we've stuck to those guns the entire time.

The lessons I've learned in Pop+Dutch's kitchen alone could fill a trilogy. For starters, do you have any idea how many ways there are to hurt yourself in a restaurant? Did you know that people can be allergic to sorghum? Have you ever fixed a three-bay sink that was draining all over the floor of the kitchen during a Bear Week lunch rush while there is a camera crew filming you for a news story about Provincetown? Are you aware that the health inspector usually comes during the busiest week in July? Have you ever confronted how long it takes to boil water in a pot the size of your body on an induction burner? Does the process of cleaning an industrial meat slicer haunt your sleep? Have you ever, for some godforsaken reason, decided to host a crawfish boil *inside?*

Owning a restaurant for the first time is kind of like skydiving for the first time — you can try to prepare, you can read a lot, and you can practice for the real thing, but in the end, you just figure it out while it's happening, or you die.

As customers go, the bad eggs make the lovely ones stand out, of course. Like Jimmy and Ezra, who we can always count on to bring a tin can full of flowers from their garden a few times a month, fervently preach the gospel of our biscuits, and repay us with some of the most elaborate and luxurious dinner parties I've ever attended in my life.

Little Ricky, who takes a vegetarian Italian combo down to his bench in front of the Coast Guard station several times a week and is one of the only people alive who I consensually allow to call me "Becky." Mark, who brings his infectious smile in for iced coffee at least once a day before he takes his dog Bailey for a walk, who we can count on to try every weird special we can think of. Maria, who we lovingly refer to as the Mayor of Provincetown, who rides her bike in a mini skirt during every season and temperature, knows the name of every single service worker in Provincetown, and always cheers us up just by laughing once.

It's undeniable that the friendships I've made in kitchens, restaurant or otherwise, are some of the longest-lasting and intense ones of my life, and with good reason. Restaurant friendships are forged in sweat and adrenaline. It might seem silly or surprising, or like the stakes aren't really that high, but you would only believe that if you'd never stared down 40 breakfast tickets at once on an 85 degree day in July, with hungover Circuit Boys stalking around the outside of your shop like wolves in striped tank tops who thirst for cold brew. Hungry people are some of the least reasonable on Earth, and negotiating their order with them is truly not for the faint of heart. Pop+Dutch wouldn't have survived a single season be it not for the friendly band of mercenary perverts we recruited along the way.

They're each owed their due for keeping us sane and alive:

Brendan, who crashed through the first few summers with us, helping us figure out a vegan cookie that people would actually eat, always spending way too long on the chalkboard drawings, and getting startled by the mere sight of someone in his peripheral vision.

Joe, the hot, tender, unbelievably loud attorney who (in addition to always managing to feed us something after-hours when we needed it the most) pinch-hits for us during busy weeks so perennially that I think the entire staff thinks of him as their hilarious, grumpy uncle.

Dori, who taught me everything I know about laughing while you watch the world burn, the grave importance of a beet when you're hungover, and the power of unexpected tahini.

Mony, who holds the record for being able to cashier for the longest without losing her entire mind, and then manages to go play like three gigs a night.

Alexandrina, who stole our towels and our hearts, and is probably going to go on to solve world hunger or something.

June, our silent assassin, who keeps quiet right up until she absolutely skewers someone and brings us all to our knees with laughter.

Gary, our original Papi, beloved to every single regular, our pint-sized ray of sunshine (until you piss him off), who glows like a lightning bug when you jokingly threaten him with a knife first thing in the morning.

Cristina, who looks like a ballerina from heaven and talks like Werner Herzog and would hands-down be my choice if I needed someone to join me in a knife fight.

Sofia, whose brain has become an extension of mine in that shop, does some of the fastest, cleanest prep I've ever seen in a restaurant, can draw anything you can imagine on demand (including, once, a seagull with an olive for a head), and has more desire to try new things than anyone I've ever met.

Catherine, who taught us all more than we ever bargained for about The Great Molasses Flood of 1918, and gently reminded us all that you can give great service without caring whether your clientele live or die.

Mackenzie, our stunning drag giraffe, who worked more jobs than anyone not on a J-1 Visa ever has, and still managed to be authentically kind and gentle to every single person who walked through the door.

Kelly, who never had any business working in a shop as janky as ours but fit in so immediately and taught us all so much in such a short period of time that she should get royalties from us for the rest of our lives.

The ones I'm forgetting, either by accident or on purpose, who inevitably did something so funny or stupid that I'm sure I will wake up someday soon in the middle of the night and curse myself for not including them.

They all have their strengths and weaknesses. I've learned to spot them quickly, and fit people in where they fit best, rather than trying to struggle against the tide. You learn things about people in a kitchen fast — what foods they love and hate, who their ex-partner is, where they grew up, who they despise, who they miss, what they want for family meal, which salad they hate prepping and which they love, what song they absolutely cannot listen to, and what their face looks like when they're hitting their limit for being nice in public.

However, hands-down, one of the most universal experiences in any kitchen has to be reckoning with The Tyranny of "Umm ... "

You may think that this is an innocuous syllable. You may think it's a vocal tic that people employ unconsciously while they gather their thoughts. Then you, my friend, have never worked in a restaurant kitchen.

"Umm ... " can be the leading introduction to literally anything. Sometimes it's simple — "Umm ... Rebecca, the produce delivery is here." Sometimes it's a confession — "Umm ... so, I dropped a quart of marinated artichoke hearts in the walk-in." Sometimes it's catastrophic — "Umm ... can one of you guys take over while I get the burn cream out of the first aid kit?" Sometimes it's gossip — "Umm ... did you guys see how drunk that guy still was?"

"Umm ... " I hear it behind me at least five times per day.

"Umm ... " I've heard it so much from each one of them, that I've begun to be able to guess by the inflection whether it's serious or not.

"Umm ... " I take a deep breath, brace myself for impact.

"Umm ... " I hear it in my work-stress dreams that invariably arrive in late June, as we gear up for the Fourth of July madness.

"Umm ... " I hear a barista say in a coffee shop I don't even own and begin to panic for whomever they're talking to.

The only thing more certain than hearing that syllable, is that it will eventually be followed by the revelation that someone is hurt. No one ever wants to gravely injure themselves in a restaurant, but odds are, it's going to happen sooner or later. Everything is hot. Everything has a sharp edge. Everyone steps backward at the worst possible time, no matter how insistently you yell "behind!" Everything is heavier than you thought it would be. But you need only cut your finger open on the line to watch how much the people around you care.

Someone always goes back to your station to grab the knife and sanitize it. Someone pulls down the first aid kit while you wash your hands. Someone wraps gauze and blue tape around it. Someone hands you an orange juice. Then they all go back to work until you're back to normal. It's always felt really silly to compare this to battle, but I'd go to war for these people. Or at least portion the butter for them.

Pop+Dutch Biscuits

adapted from the *Pop+Dutch Snackbook, Vol. 1*

In the early days, I used to weigh 12 oz. blocks of butter, freeze them, and grate them every morning to make the biscuits. This resulted, as you might expect, in roughly 300 scraped knuckles and a very sore arm. Along the way, one of our good eggs said, "why don't you just grate the butter and freeze it?" Now, there's an entire chest freezer dedicated to holding portioned bags of frozen butter. This recipe, which I adapted from the Tupelo Honey Cafe's killer biscuit, makes 12 buttery lumps of joy with no more knuckle injuries. I like to keep a bag of grated butter in the freezer all the time, just in case you wake up in the morning and need biscuits.

12 oz. unsalted butter, grated, tossed with a bit of flour and frozen
4 cups flour
2 Tbsp. baking powder
½ tsp. baking soda
3 ½ tsp. salt
4 Tbsp. sour cream
2 cups buttermilk
2 Tbsp. butter, melted

Preheat oven to 450°F.

Combine the flour, baking powder, baking soda, and salt in a large bowl. Add the sour cream and cut into the flour with a fork. Add your frozen, grated butter and toss to coat. Quickly cut the butter into the flour mixture with a pastry cutter or your hands, until the mixture resembles coarse meal (butter should be roughly the size of large peas).

Add the buttermilk to the flour mixture and stir just until it starts to come together. Fold the dough over on itself a few times, so the wet bits pick up the dry bits. (Shhh, biscuit dough is supposed to look ugly.)
On a floured surface, turn out the dough and GENTLY pat out to a 1" thick rectangle. Cut into 12 biscuits and place, almost touching, on a rimmed baking sheet.

Cook in the upper third of the oven for about 10 minutes. Turn the tray and go seven minutes longer — or until light brown. Brush biscuits with melted butter and return to the oven for two minutes, until golden.

Makes 12 biscuits

Provincetown: Just Brian Being Brian

One of the dumbest things I ever heard someone say out loud was about the tide. It was summertime, and I was taking a lunch break on the beach deck behind the sandwich shop. This is always a dangerous proposition – on the one hand, you get to feel the sun, look at the water, smell the beach roses, which is a rare treat for those of us who work on the schedule of the tourist economy; on the other hand, it means that people can talk to you.

In this case I was lucky. This person was talking to his friends and not directly to me, so I only had to *overhear* one of the dumbest things I've ever heard; I didn't have to interact with it. There were three of them – tan, toned, middle-aged men, with the gentlest sag to their arm skin, betraying the youth they'd paid to have reapplied to their faces. They were lined up in Adirondack chairs on the furthest edge of the deck, closest to the bayside beach, drinking cartoonishly large glasses of white wine. This is a pretty familiar scene with very familiar players. It gets to the point during the height of the summer where I know how someone will order based on what kind of tank top they're wearing. You grow to love and despise them. Sometimes they surprise you, for better or worse.

I was not eavesdropping, but it was impossible to ignore, both because of the content and the volume.

"Wait, I have a question," the one in the middle began, putting his arms out to either side, to silence all further discussion. "Last time we were out here, it was super full, and now it's almost empty."

"What?" To be fair, the one on the left was correct. What? There's not a much better invitation to what came next.

"The water," he explained, "there was so much of it before."

"It's ... just ... the tide," the one on the right offered cautiously, like when a child mentions their imaginary friend and you have to figure out whether they are actually seeing a ghost. "The tide went out."

"But where does it go? Does it, like, drain?"

They laughed a laugh that smacked of "Just Brian being Brian!" I didn't hear what happened next, because it becomes very difficult to hear when your brain is leaking out of your ears.

What would you do if your friend said something like this to you? In that moment, I wanted to pour his glass of wine over his head, to scream at him for wasting his short time on this planet being so moronic, to ask how he made it this far, to demand to know how his friends put up with this, why they would travel with someone like this, if they could stand it.

Right now, I think I'd want to protect him.

I heard Neil Degrasse Tyson explain once, that the tide doesn't come "in and out." He said that there is a bulge of water surrounding our planet, protruding out further on either side because of gravity and orbital force, and we spin within it. We come to the tide. We leave it. It waits there for us. We catch up to it. It's too much to think about for too long. It makes my head want to explode, but I suspect Brian would think, "oh, okay sure," and refill his wine glass.

It's hard to know how to protect people right now.

There were days during the pandemic that felt like whole three-act plays. There were days that were really fucking raw, both indoors and outdoors. For you too, I bet.

Every time I sat down to write during that time, I ended up circling back to soothing us somehow. Then, at a certain point, it became apparent that we were going to have to start thinking about the future again, in a way that I hadn't permitted myself to for a while. It hurt. It required some time to adjust. It required that we protect each other rather than judge each other. It required compassion. It was a lot to ask of ourselves, to ask of each other. But we had to try. It still requires some effort. It's foolish to apply this sentiment to everyone, of course, especially in a world where Ted Cruz still exists, but we have to try to assume that the people around us are really trying their best, and give them some extra room to fuck up, to fumble, to ask a really stupid question.

Delving deep into empathy and exercising compassion for things and people that annoy or disturb us can really take a lot out of your gas tank. It's in these moments I remember that we also need to eat a vegetable. That's just a fact. I'm here to help with that.

Rice and Lettuce Soup

This recipe is adapted from Tamar Adler's An Everlasting Meal, *a book which I have given as a gift so many times, I have occasionally tried to give it to someone twice. She describes this dish as "truly pacifying," which is exactly what we need right now. In her words: "I passed this recipe along to a friend who reported that it was 'butter's highest and best use, because the lettuce becomes an expression of butter... sweet, crunchy, innocent butter.'"*

2 small onions, diced
2 Tbsp. unsalted butter
⅓ c. parsley leaves, roughly chopped
½ c. arborio rice
2 quarts chicken or vegetable stock (homemade kicks ass, but it doesn't need to be)
1 very big head Romaine lettuce, cut into fine ribbons
Good olive oil for serving
Salt and black pepper to taste

Cook the onions in the butter in a large pot over medium heat, salting them once you've added them to the pot. When they're softened and getting translucent, add the parsley and cook for another minute or two. Add the rice and liquid, and let simmer for about half an hour, until the rice is completely cooked through, and then for another 20 minutes, until it goes jagged around the edges (I continue to be obsessed with the wording of this direction). Turn off the heat. Taste for salt and pepper. When you're ready to eat, warm the soup up, add the lettuce to the soup, and mix it through. Serve each bowl with rice mounded in the middle and more liquid poured over. Drizzle with good olive oil and crack fresh pepper over it.

Serves 4

Ticonderoga: Cold Cuts

My parents always worked in tandem in the kitchen – my dad was often the one doing the dishes after my mom made the food, but they both had their own particular specialties. I'm startled to realize that I have never seen either of my grandfathers cook anything – although, to be fair, I've never really seen my mom's mother cook anything either.

In Ina and Jay's kitchen in Staten Island, New York – the house my mom grew up in where Ina still lives – the only things we ever prepared for ourselves were sandwiches from cold cuts in the fridge, hot water in the kettle for "tea balls," as she has always called tea bags, and whatever mystifying combination of leftovers my uncles cobbled together for their idiosyncratic breakfasts. I have a distinct memory of one of them making a cold spaghetti sandwich once, while I looked on in genuine confusion, sipping my glass of Apple & Eve apple juice. This appears to be canon for this part of the family – my mom recalls with visible discomfort the time Ina made "American Chop Suey," which she described as leftover Chinese noodles topped with mashed potatoes like some kind of unholy Shepherd's Pie. What we ate in the house on Albert Street was mostly a function of my parents really missing Chinese take-out and Jewish deli food.

The first night on any visit to Staten Island there was always a banquet of roast pork lo mein, wonton soup, BBQ spareribs in the foil-lined paper bag, egg rolls and enough spicy mustard to kill a man. My mom would dance around humming in her chair like she does when she's happy, and my dad would crack jokes with my uncles. When he was still around, their German shorthair pointer, Willie, would sprawl out under the glass-topped dining room table, waiting for someone to drop something. The table was just slightly too big for the space it was in, so that we always had to wait for my grandfather to sit down at the head of the table closest to the window, lest we all have to get up to let him in. I was always afraid I'd put my glass down too hard on that table and crack it and couldn't imagine why anyone would choose that for themselves. It is still in Ina's dining room to this day. It's where she drinks her tea, paints her watercolors, and reads the newspaper that she will not remember reading.

The next day we would usually go to Golden's Deli on the other side of the island — a very typical Kosher deli made extraordinary by the most hilarious restaurant gimmick I've ever seen: an actual vintage subway car parked right in the middle of the restaurant. Golden's, like other delis of its ilk, had a relish bar, where you could pile a plate with creamy coleslaw, full and half-sour pickles, pickled green tomatoes, and giardiniera. My mom always got a corned beef and chopped liver sandwich on rye, and my dad would distress the entire table with his signature order: a cup of kasha varnishkes to start (farfalle pasta tossed with schmaltzed buckwheat and onions), and a steaming plate of stuffed derma, which is basically Ashkenazi haggis, draped in gravy. He graciously let me try a taste of it before explaining what it was, so that I knew it was delicious before I understood that it is matzo-meal stuffing poached in a beef intestine.

"Old world comfort food," he said, smiling, as if he had ever been in any way associated with the old world.

Visiting Ina and Jay always felt a little bit strange. My brother and I spent so much time with Norm and Glenda, my dad's parents, that they became an extension of our nuclear family. We only saw my mom's parents and brothers, Jeff and Jamie, once a year — sometimes even less frequently than that. My mom was always a little anxious before these trips, in a way I understand so intimately now that I am an adult. She was worried about how much Ina would worry, and she certainly did: She worried that the bath water was too hot or not hot enough; she worried that I'd catch my fingers in the pull-out sofa I slept on in my grandpa's office (which I did, every time); she worried that we hadn't had enough to eat, or that we might want to take a walk in the park across the street. Ina is a kind, intelligent woman, who has spent an incredible amount of her life tending to the needs of people who were frequently irritated by her concern. She loves dogs, art museums, and purple irises, and I often wonder what her life would have been like if she were married to someone who wasn't my grandfather.

The times when we were together outside the Albert Street house always felt a little lighter. Once, Jamie invited us to visit him and his girlfriend at their summer share in Point Pleasant, New Jersey (yes, I mean proto-Jersey shore — they were wearing acid washed jeans and there was at least one mullet). My dad carried me on his shoulders down the boardwalk, and Jamie showed me how to shake malt vinegar onto a cone of fries for the very first time.

We also spent a lot of time together at my great-grandparents' summer house. This house, wrapped in a screened porch, perched on a little hill right on the shore of Lake George still stands today, almost exactly as it was when Great-Grandma Zu and Great-Grandpa Si were alive. When my grandmother dies, it will officially belong to my uncles and their families, although they've been the ones who have taken care of it, loved it, and argued over it for my entire life.

I was too young to really have a full picture of my great-grandparents as they were — in my own mythology they were both born in Russia and left to escape the Holocaust — which as it turns out is 100% incorrect. Simon (my grandmother's second husband) was born in Pennsylvania and Zu was born in London. I'm named after Zu, but I didn't know her name was Rebecca until well after she died. I have been told for my entire life, and I will die on this hill — that we called her Zu because her family escaped the Nazis to go live with the Zulus in South Africa, which I have recently learned is absolute bullshit. We, in fact, called her Zu because her father fought in the Boer War *on the English side,* which is an excellent lesson that if you, as a white person, even one from a marginalized community, scratch just below the surface of your family's history, you will always find colonialism there, one way or another. This wrong story I believed for so long, of course makes no sense, since by 1939 Rebecca Birch and Simon Hillman were already living in New York together, since my grandfather who went on to serve in WWII had already been born in 1923 — actual details of actual history can feel so distant when you have a romantic idea in your head.

There are, as it turns out, a relatively gigantic number of things I never knew about these people. I had always known that Si was Zu's second husband. I knew that my Great-Grandpa Nathan, her first husband, had died, and that she remarried Si, "their best friend," shortly thereafter. Within 24 hours of my coming out to my mom as polyamorous, she admitted that there was more to the story all along. Si was not just their best friend; he lived with them for years and years, even had his own bedroom in the Ticonderoga house, which was linked by a secret hallway to the bathroom and the primary bedroom.

In order to get the picture, you need only look at actual pictures of the family. My Great-Grandpa Nathan, and Great-Uncle Murph, both of whom died before I was born, look exactly the same. Great-Grandpa Si, who my Grandpa Jay always, *always* referred to as his stepfather, are unmistakably kin. It may be hard for you to imagine no one ever bringing this up — it is for me too, except that these are people who treat conversations about emotions like ritualistic torture. To wit: I recently asked my mother point-blank whether or not these people were living in an openly polyamorous, non-traditional family structure, co-parenting their collective children in harmony.

"Yes, but please don't write about it," she said. "My brothers would be so embarrassed."

My mother and I do not have the type of relationship that allows me to immediately express to her how hurtful and offensive it is to categorize the relationship style I've chosen for myself as a dark, unbreachable family secret meant to be left behind in history, and I suspect it will take me some time to unpack that one. But it feels a little too on-the-nose that this woman — *my namesake* — was potentially so like me and had potentially cracked a code that I feel like I'm still actively deciphering. There are things about the love between Zu, Nat, and Si that I will never know, because there's no one really left to ask.

The Ticonderoga house is the only place where I ever really knew them, and whenever we were there, before I was even 10, I was a little scared of their age. They were the oldest people I had ever known, and I was afraid they wouldn't be able to hear me, that I wouldn't understand them, that we'd be mysteries to each other. There, in that house on Lake George, all I wanted to do was make clover flower crowns in the yard, fish for minnows off the dock, write secret messages on pieces of birch bark, pick blueberries off the bushes in the driveway, and insist that I absolutely did not want my dad and uncles to teach me to water-ski. On our way there, we would always stop at the grocery store in Lake George Village — my mom and I would buy the biggest bag of cheese curds we could find, and we'd make sure there were donuts to put in the tin breadbox at home, cold-cuts for the fridge (this family mostly gathers together when there is sliced meat on the table), and enough fodder to keep whoever manned the little BBQ grill on the back porch busy for hours.

When Zu was alive, there were little crystal dishes all over the house filled with candy — gum drops, those ubiquitous strawberry bon-bons that no one has ever known the names of, and hard candies shaped like raspberries. My mom says that when she was my age, Zu used to give her a highball of scotch and ginger ale to put her to sleep, but I never got to experience that tradition.

There was a great big, enameled stove in the little green linoleum-tiled kitchen that lit up in rainbow colors when you turned it on, and my mom swears it used to sing to you when it was brand new and top-of-the-line. Breakfast was always a big production there, and something I got to help with — lining the bacon slices up on paper towels, cracking a dozen eggs into a bowl, pouring orange juice into a glass pitcher. I was always unnerved by how I could feel the floors creak under my feet in that house, having grown up in a one-story house in the desert with no basement. I hated how hollow it felt, knowing that there were floors below and above, how I couldn't get up to pee in the middle of the night without waking the whole house.

I was the first grandkid in the family, so I was something of a commodity and a curiosity on both sides. It meant that my Uncle Jamie laughed at every joke I made and would always make a stupid face into the camera with me, that my Uncle Jeff, the oldest brother, taught me how to drive the boat while I sat on his lap, that I always got to snuggle with the dog, that Jeff's wife, my aunt Ellen, would send me a neon bathing suit before the trip and play Barbies with me in the yard. I was charmed, and it was charming, and I feel lucky to have gotten to experience those people in that way, while they were all so young and mostly being kind to each other.

I remember spending hours fishing off the dock with my grandfather, but I don't think we ever cooked anything we caught. My grandfather wouldn't eat fish, unless it was broiled filet of sole in lemon and butter, and in that house, no one ever did anything Jay didn't want them to. He was a gruff, stubborn person, who smiled biggest when he was joking at someone else's expense — his three grandchildren all called him "Grumpy." Once, after a long visit with them in New York, he wrote me a letter about how much he loved me and how much the time we spent together had meant to him. It made my mom sob uncontrollably, and I was so lucky to not be able to understand why at the time. I never had any question about how much love there was for me while I grew up, and I had no idea how hard some people have to fight for that feeling, if they can ever get it at all.

Provincetown: Ecco!

It's hard not to get angry when I think of you. I've tried a lot — to stop, to act like I don't care, to act like you never existed, to act like walking past you on the street doesn't make my guts ache with regret. It might make it easier for both of us if this were true. But of course, it isn't. It's hard not to think of you today, because you've just announced that you're leaving. It's stupid that you even get to be in this book.

In truth, I think about you almost every day. I think about you when I pass the places you've lived, when I pass the two empty storefronts that once held your shop, when I get ready to open my own for the season. I think of you while I decide what to make for dinner when I have company, and when I decide what to call a new sandwich at Pop+Dutch, and when I pass you on your way to the post office, dragging your once-handsome, now-disintegrating boots across the sidewalk, in a stained sweatshirt and what is probably a vintage Hermès scarf, arms laden with packages for who knows who. In those moments, it's impossible to forget that you exist, even if I'd be happier if I could.

In truth, some of the best meals I ever ate were in your kitchen. Well, not your kitchen, per se, but the kitchen where you cooked us all those tremendous, improbable meals on that ancient cast iron stove, with the tiny oven compartment that burnt your hand every time you grabbed the handle.

In truth, the idea for this book came to me after one of those nights around that candlelit table, on the mostly broken antique chairs, after drinking wine from those enormous, vintage crystal goblets. I thought about how so many of my most important memories were around a dinner table, and how the most important conversations, the clearest epiphanies, and the moments I've fallen in love have always been in — or because of — a kitchen. You probably made us a stew of braised pork, hacked into chunks on the bone, in a gravy so infuriatingly delicious — infuriating because I can always figure out the ingredients to any dish I love, but yours were often so elusive, and so frustratingly simple once you'd finally reveal what they were to me with a grin and a flourish of your hand, an Italian finger purse punctuating each syllable.

"Ecco!" You'd shout, whenever I finally got the point that the applesauce was just apples and apples alone, or when I summarized your paragraph-long rant about a person — about how tedious they were — down to one sentence, or when I asked the right question when we were trying to figure something out. You're not Italian, but you put this persona on when you really want to make a point, because you have loved so many elder Italian ladies, and because you take them more seriously than you take most people, and because this cheeky and easy bravado helps to hide some of the deep self-loathing that sometimes escapes around your edges when you get upset.

I knew while we were friends that you thought of me like a child, and I guess part of me liked to have an adult around.

Both of our dads died way before they should have, and long before we were ready for them to, and I think the way we miss and revere them made us feel closer to each other than we were to other people. Then your older brother died, and then your mom, and eventually a million more people in the awful years that came after, and you started to get mad at me for not having as much space for you as I once did. But you didn't tell me that until it was already too late, direct confrontation never really being your thing, until you've already gotten so mad that your jaw stays clenched shut when you speak.

There are myriad ways in which I miss you, and myriad ways in which I don't. Because human beings are absurd, those often exist in the same spaces. I miss the hours at Pop+Dutch that you would sit in the kitchen while we worked and read us things from the newspaper. I don't miss how exasperated you would get when I asked you to move so I could open the oven. I miss sitting with you at the counter for a few minutes when things slowed down, and talking about what the day would bring. I don't miss when you would bring up someone you wanted to be nasty about, "How's your dear friend, _____?" I miss your feedback on the crumb of the focaccia and the texture of the biscuits, how you celebrated each new jam flavor, and always wanted to eat a ham and butter sandwich in the morning. I don't miss when I would refer to it as a restaurant, and you would say, about the place you ate 50% of your meals for six months of the year, "Well, it's not really a *restaurant,* is it?"

I always thought it was funny when you'd exclaim: "None of you people give me enough respect," right up until I realized you were actually serious. That's when lots of things I brushed off as silly little annoyances became painfully pointed.

You already know all of the ways I feel about all of the things you said to end our friendship. I'm sad that you're leaving, and my instinct since I found out has been to want to call you to apologize for how things ended between us, but I've decided I'm not going to apologize to men anymore for things they've done to hurt me. You were part of what made this place feel like my home for a really long time. I hope, wherever you go next, you find a place to be happier. It will be nice to miss you once you're gone, instead of missing you while I pass you in the street.

HOW TO SURVIVE A BREAKFAST RUSH AT POP+DUTCH

Take a deep breath.

Wash your hands.

Coffee. A whole one now, another whole one during or after.

Protein: can be cheese.

Give each other a hug first.

Make sure everyone has a count on biscuits.

Don't look behind you.

Don't listen to the questions.

Actually *read* the tickets – it's worth the extra time.

Laugh when you fuck up.

Rihanna.

Economize your movements.

Always have your towel. Make sure it is dry.

Winged eyeliner makes you look scarier than you are.

No egg whites.

Provincetown: The Truest Thing I've Ever Said

Sean was outside potentially breaking up with his long-distance girlfriend via FaceTime. He came back in after more than an hour down at the beach across from our house.

"Well," he said, "we broke up."

"Oh Bug, I'm so sorry. I didn't know what to do, so I just started making guacamole."

Truro: All Our Gardens

A few weeks after cherry tomatoes brought my tastebuds back to life from Covid, Sean and I were out to dinner at one of our favorite restaurants. Terra Luna was set in an old house on the shore road just over the Truro town line. It was filled with local art and owned and run by a good friend (and fellow weirdo) who DJs on the local radio station with Sean. It has been the site of many magical evenings, many important summits, many legendary flirtations, and it was one of the only places on this spit of land that treated local mackerel with any respect.

It's busy on this particular night in late summer, as it usually is, and we get to enjoy the privilege of being recognized by the host as haggard locals. He puts us at the first two-top he has, between a trio of gray-haired, artist-looking ladies and a family that appears to be a husband and wife in their mid-30s, and two of their parents. Sean and I are already prone to eavesdropping, having been ritualistically conditioned by our writing professors to listen to real dialogue in order to write our own. It's a blessing and a curse — you catch a lot of gems, but you also catch a lot of stray bullets, and sometimes dinner is totally devoted to the insane things the next table is saying to each other. We're rendered speechless, incapable of producing our own thoughts, just widening our eyes at each other and occasionally texting across the table when it's too much to bear. Writers: We are not for everyone.

In this case, I am too hungry to listen to anyone, and am doing one-sided negotiations with Sean about what we are starting with: "I think cod cakes and artichoke pâté, but if you'd rather have sardines, I'm down. Also, it's so chilly outside I might get the duck. I never do because I think it's crazy to order that in the summer, but this feels like an exception. You're getting the stewed beans special, right? That's got your name all over it."

Once I run out of breath, I look up to meet Sean's gaze, his eyes like saucers over his cocktail, looking at me with urgency as he sips. His eyes flick quickly, almost imperceptibly to the left, and I realize I've missed something significant at the next table. The corners of my mouth creep upward into a smirk while he pulls his phone out of his pocket to send me a message from one and a half feet away, by now the steps of this wordless tango are familiar choreography to me.

My phone lights up: "The father-in-law, as the son-in-law offered photos of his garden: 'Well, you don't have kids, so you have tomatoes'."

Before I can stop myself, I have gasped audibly. The sound makes us both laugh, and I stare back at the menu with my eyes bulging.

To some people this comment might feel innocuous (maybe even encouraging to some of you freaks), but Sean and I think otherwise. I know that we agree without having to ask. This is partially informed by my heritage — I was fluent in sarcasm before I could read — but it's also my biology. As a person with a uterus, who is theoretically capable of gestating a new person, lots of people have opinions about how soon I should use it to do so.

For a long time, there was no question in my mind that I would. I love kids — I love watching them learn things; I love when they accidentally teach you things; I love when they surprise you by knowing more than they should; I love watching them be curious and strange. Sean and I have one nephew and one niece so far (and one new, undoubtedly strange little nibling on the way). Spending time with them has made me remember how true all of this is, and that my decision to keep my uterus tenant-free isn't because of the end result. I think Sean and I would be great parents. I think we'd raise a strange, generous, curious person. And I think I might be beside myself the entire time.

I'm an anxious person, mostly about the health and safety of the people I love. My history has taught me that we're not owed one more single day, and that chance can swing all too swiftly against you. In some ways I think it would have been easier for me to decide to have kids when I was younger, before I understood consequences this well, and before I'd experienced really heavy losses. If I'm honest, I think this world as it stands today (and stands to become in the near future) is too awful for me to be able to relax at all while keeping an adorable genetic copy of ourselves alive. I know I'd fall in love with whatever peanut grew in my belly, and I know that the potential to lose them might break me.

And so, we have tomatoes.

I know that doesn't sound particularly cheerful, and I know it doesn't sound like I'm much fun at parties, but I promise you that I have started to find some joy in this decision, and that I am actually very fun, especially if there is punch. This is a decision that Sean and I came to together, after many years of swinging back and forth. We haven't always agreed — there was a time not too long ago when I felt absolutely ready to take the plunge. He wasn't, and I resented it. It was a heavy burden to carry together for a while. Particularly heartbreaking was the moment I looked at the shelf of children's books I'd been collecting for decades and realized that I wasn't saving those for anyone in particular anymore.

Those books are still here, and so are we, and I'll confess to feeling liberated in knowing that they don't have to go anywhere if I don't want them to. That they can come along with us on whatever part of the journey comes next. To rest alongside whatever cookbooks we collect, on whatever shelf in whatever house we end up in next, to feed whichever people we love the most right then. They can get sent to new little people and their parents, or they can just continue to be mine. To be loved for what they taught me when I was small and weird and curious.

The louder I get about being queer and polyamorous, the less people seem to feel licensed to interrogate my procreational choices. This is a selfish relief. It does nothing to protect other people with theoretical gestational capabilities (I say so over and over again because usually the U.S. healthcare system won't even let you check to see if you're *able* to get pregnant unless you are *actively trying to!*). It protects me from having to have hard conversations with friends and family about climate disaster and nihilism that they are almost certainly not ready to have — so in a way, I guess it protects them too. But it also indicts the kinds of behavior our society expects of women in relationships in the middle of their lives. When I'm presenting heteronormatively, I'm expected to make new people. I'm often pitied or resented if I don't. When I'm not, those expectations shift rapidly. If you are the kind of person who feels comfortable asking someone "when are you going to have kids?" I hope you spend some time asking yourself why you think that's appropriate, who you feel most compelled to ask, and why it even matters to you.

This decision often gets conflated with judgment — *because I am not going to have kids, I must think no one should, right?* Absolutely not. I mean, I think a lot of you shouldn't, but I don't think *none* of you should. I've tumbled this boulder over in my mind so many times, I could fit it into a ring setting, and I think where I've landed is that making and raising kids, if you are able to make your own choice about it, is a choice that you make for yourself. It's about what you want for your life, and how you want it to look. It's about what *you* want to experience, not necessarily about wanting a new person to get to experience life. And that, I realized with somewhat embarrassing surprise, is actually a fine thing to be selfish about.

In the end, not having to think about this question anymore gives me a lot more room to think about what I want the rest of my life to look like, and what actually gives me pleasure. It gives me a lot more time to plan the menu. To invite the loved ones. To feed us. To enjoy us in the moment. To clink glasses. To tend to the tomatoes.

What kind should we grow next year?

Provincetown: The Pit of the Mango

He always saves me the pit of the mango
To eat over the sink
And let the juice run down my arm.
I have to floss afterward, but it's worth it.
It's kind of like tasting the sun and a beautiful girl
And he always lets me be the one to do it.

Acknowledgements

To Sean, who always knew I could write this and always makes me a cocktail right when I need one.

To Patrick Davis at Unbound Edition Press, for believing I could take this book off my brain, and to Cory Firestine, for finding the fine lines.

To Flynn, for being my co-conspirator and forever editor.

To Jason, for telling our mom about that grape, and for being all the best things about our parents, combined.

To Digby Wolfe, for reminding me to do what I'm good at, even when it seems impractical, and for insisting that if I wouldn't marry him, I should try it out with Sean.

To Ashleigh, Alison, Tyler, Joe, Adam, Claire, Ellery, Kelly, Julian, Dori, Daniil, Gary, Ben, Tess, Kiah, Cody, Casey, Mama T, Kevin, Chris, Jake, Marcy, Jim, Dr. Booze, JSuh and Luke — you're chosen family I would choose again and again.

To Erykah Badu, Big Thief, Big Maybelle, Dijon, Blossom Dearie, Alabaster Deplume, Ruth Brown, Hiatus Kaiyote, Kate Bollinger, Ella Fitzgerald, The A's, Waxahatchee, Michael Hurley, and The Supremes, all of whose music guided me through finding these words.

To Joan Didion and M.F.K. Fisher, without whom I wouldn't have realized that people even want to read books like this.

About the Author

Rebecca Orchant is the Co-Owner of Pop+Dutch, a sandwich shop and curiosities market in Provincetown, MA, where she has lived year-round with her husband Sean since 2014. Formerly a Food Editor at *The Huffington Post,* Orchant also performs burlesque as The Duchess of Sandwich, is currently the Vice Chair of the board of The Provincetown Commons, and contributes to *The Provincetown Independent*. She was born and raised in Albuquerque, NM, and received a BFA in Dramatic Writing from The University of New Mexico, where she received a regional award, and was a national finalist for the John Cauble Award for Outstanding Short Play from The Kennedy Center American College Theatre Festival. She is probably thinking about cheese right now.

About the Type and Paper

Designed by Malou Verlomme of the Monotype Studio, Macklin is an elegant, high-contrast typeface. It has been designed purposely for more emotional appeal.

The concept for Macklin began with research on historical material from Britain and Europe dating to the beginning of the 19th century, specifically the work of Vincent Figgins. Verlomme pays respect to Figgins's work with Macklin, but pushes the family to a more contemporary place.

This book is printed on natural Rolland Enviro Book stock. The paper is 100 percent post-consumer sustainable fiber content and is FSC-certified.

Simmering was designed by Eleanor Safe and Joseph Floresca.

Unbound Edition Press champions honest, original voices. Committed to the power of writers who explore and illuminate the contemporary human condition, we publish collections of poetry, short fiction, and essays. Our publisher and editorial team aim to identify, develop, and defend authors who create thoughtfully challenging work which may not find a home with mainstream publishers. We are guided by a mission to respect and elevate emerging, under-appreciated, and marginalized authors, with a strong commitment to advancing LGBTQ+ and BIPOC voices. We are honored to make meaningful contributions to the literary arts by publishing their work.

unboundedition.com